The Essential
Advent and Christmas
Handbook

7/21

The Essential Advent and Christmas Handbook

A DAILY COMPANION WITH A GLOSSARY OF KEY TERMS

A REDEMPTORIST PASTORAL PUBLICATION

Liguori
LIGUORI, MISSOURI

Imprimi Potest:
Richard Thibodeau, C.Ss.R.
Provincial, Denver Province
The Redemptorists

Published by Liguori Publications
Liguori, Missouri
www.liguori.org

Library of Congress Cataloging-in-Publication Data

Santa, Thomas M.
    The essential Advent and Christmas handbook : a daily companion : with a glossary of key terms /compiled by Thomas M. Santa, C.Ss.R.—1st ed.
      p. cm.
    ISBN 978-0-7648-0661-2 (pbk.)
    1. Advent—Prayer-books and devotions—English. 2. Christmas—Prayer-books and devotions—English. 3. Catholic Church—Prayer-books and devotions—English. I. Santa, Thomas M., 1952– . II. Series.

BX2170.A4 E88 2000
242'.33—dc21   00–35212

Acknowledgments

This handbook would not have been possible without the contributions of the members of the Redemptorist Pastoral Publication team at Liguori Publications and publications staff at Liguori Publication. Each contributed to this collection in his or her own special way. Father Paul Coury, C.Ss.R., and Brother Dan Korn, C.Ss.R., need to be singled out for praise; each of them contributed to this handbook the fruits of their own reflections and prayers. It is our hope that this handbook is useful to each person on his or her spiritual journey. Perhaps, as a result of this effort, your celebration of the Advent-Christmas season will be a time of blessing for you and for the members of your family.

Contents

Contents

Contents

Contents

Section Twelve: Family Meal Prayers for the Holiday Season 239

Section Thirteen: Glossary of Key Terms 257

Sources 269

How to Use This Book

This handbook is conceived as an essential reference for the reader's spiritual preparation for the season of Advent. In addition to resources particular to Advent, we have collected appropriate spiritual aids that will help the reader in the spiritual celebration of the Church's liturgical season as it continues from the feast of Christmas through the Sunday after Epiphany—the feast of the Baptism of Our Lord. Every effort has been made to collect in one volume the prayers, practices, and customs, in short all that may be needed, in order to provide you with the opportunity to journey with the Lord through the Advent and Christmas seasons. You will have your choice of prayers and devotions that are understood in the best sense as traditional, many of which are prayers that are hundreds of years old. In addition, you will be introduced to prayers and devotions that are modern, contemporary expressions of ancient themes and truths.

Central to this collection is a series of daily meditations, based on the liturgical cycle and traditional devotional themes, providing an opportunity to journey through the season with Scripture. The contemporary meditations presented in this book weave story, anecdote, and practical wisdom together in order to provide a springboard for private prayer and meditation. The traditional meditations included here are by the great Saint and Doctor of the Church, Saint Alphonsus Liguori, who is often referenced as the "Preacher of the Infant Jesus," because of his extensive writings on the Incarnation of the Word of God. In addition to these meditations, many other devotional pieces commemorating the saints of the season are also included.

Because this collection is a representative sampling of that which is old and that which is new, suggestions for how to proceed may be useful. What follows are two "maps" that may be helpful in charting your personal Advent-Christmas spiritual journey plus one "map" for a family journey that can be led by an appointed member of the family group.

The Traditional Model: In this plan, an emphasis is placed on using the resources provided that are time tested and true. The presumption of the traditional plan is that repetition is useful and productive in the spiritual journey.

First thing in the morning, pray, from Section One: "Getting Started," the traditional morning prayer. This traditional devotional will provide you with step-by-step instructions and an opportunity to use the meditations of Saint Alphonsus for your spiritual journey. At some time during the day, perhaps in the afternoon when you are able to get a few moments of quiet, read from Section Five, number 10 (for Advent) and Section Nine, number 8 (for Christmas), the appropriate "Visit to the Blessed Sacrament." Ideally, of course, you would be in the presence of the Blessed Sacrament when you pray this prayer, but it is not essential. Each evening, before you retire for the night, return to Section One and pray the traditional evening prayer. When the appropriate time is presented, use the examination of conscience from Section Five, number 9, in preparation for your celebration of the sacrament of reconciliation.

The Contemporary Model: In this plan, an emphasis is placed on the resources provided that may be categorized as "modern." The presumption of the contemporary plan is that the meditation on the Word of God, chosen from the liturgical calendar, is the necessary starting point for your spiritual journey.

First thing in the morning, read the assigned Scripture passages and meditation provided from Section Six (for Advent) or Section Eleven "Contemporary Meditations" (for Christmas). The emphasis for your time of prayer should be on the regularity of the time chosen, the place you choose to pray, and the position you choose (that is, kneeling, sitting, or so forth), and, finally, the amount of time reserved for prayer. In this model, the discipline necessary for the spiritual journey may be discovered in the commitment made to the morning meditation. Everything else that you choose to do, such as reading additional selections provided in the handbook or adopting the habit of reading from another spiritual book in the afternoon, is chosen for the purpose of supporting or enriching the morning meditation. In the evening, before retiring, five to seven minutes of silent reflection on the day is highly recommended.

For those preferring a more structured contemporary approach, the contemporary morning and evening prayer that is provided in Section One might also prove to be useful.

The Family Model: In this plan, an emphasis is placed on the resources provided that may be used by the family as a unit. The presumption of this plan is that certain members of the family may well choose to follow the traditional, the contemporary, or some other plan for Lent, but there is also a commitment to share the spiritual journey with the rest of the family.

Essential to the family plan is a family meeting, before the First Sunday of Advent, where all members of the family have an opportunity to commit to the plan. It is important that there be a family commitment; the spiritual journey needs to be freely chosen by all; it cannot be imposed.

At the family meeting, the leader of the family group, chosen for this task, asks the individual members of the family to commit to the introduction of the Advent wreath into the daily routine of the family (Section Three, number 5), along with the daily lighting of the wreath and the appropriate prayer. In addition to the Advent wreath, there might also be a discussion about including meal prayers for the holiday season (Section Twelve) and, when appropriate, the blessing of the family Christmas tree (Section Nine, number 1).

For families who desire a little more of a commitment during this season, there might also be a discussion about the family joining together for Advent Vespers and the Advent Reconciliation Service at the local parish church. In addition, if the opportunity is provided for the Jesse tree or the giving tree, it might be helpful to determine the level of family participation. Finally, a discussion about joining together as a family for common worship on the Sundays of Advent and on Christmas day might also be useful.

The suggestions for the possible use of this handbook do not exhaust all of the possibilities or, for that matter, do not even begin to use all of the resources provided. The purpose of the suggestions is to simply provide a starting point, a place for your own creativity to be grounded.

SECTION ONE

Getting Started

Although a regular practice of morning and evening prayer is suggested as an appropriate spiritual discipline and exercise each day of the year, it is a highly recommended practice during special liturgical seasons in the Church's year. The practice of beginning and ending each day with prayer is essential for the spiritual journey.

Included in this presentation is a traditional example of morning and evening prayer that was quite popular before the beginning of the Second Vatican Council. Many of the prayers suggested would be well known by most Catholics. The contemporary example of morning and evening prayer is rooted in Scripture and is a well-known form of prayer that has become popular after Vatican II.

The choice of the traditional or contemporary model is a simple preference for one model instead of the other. Both models assume a respectful prayer posture, an experience of quiet and reflection, and appropriate opportunities for personal prayer and reflection.

1. Traditional Morning Prayer

In the name of the Father, and of the Son, and of the Holy Spirit. Amen.

Quietly place yourself in the presence of God and adore God's Holy Name.

Most holy and adorable Trinity, one God in three Persons. I believe that you are present here in this place. I adore you with the deepest humility and freely give to you, with my whole heart and soul, worship, praise, and thanksgiving.

Thank God for the gift of life, the gift of breath, and the gift of God's redeeming and everlasting love.

O my God, I humbly thank you for all that you have given to me. I realize that all that I am, all that I hope to be, and all that I ever will

3

be comes to me as a gift from you. I realize that this gift of life and of breath is completely unearned and unmerited. I give thanks and praise to you that you have created me in your image and likeness, that you have redeemed me by the precious blood of your Son, and that you have preserved me safe from all harm to the beginning of another day. I offer to you all my thoughts, words, and actions this day, and I consecrate them to the glory of your name. I ask that you accept my praise and worship, offered in the name of your Son, Jesus, for the greater glory of your name and for the salvation of all your people. Amen.

Resolve to avoid sin and to practice virtue.

Jesus, my Redeemer and my Lord, model of humanity, I resolve this day to imitate your example and to live the Gospel that you preached. With the help of your grace and the guidance of your Holy Spirit, I resolve to be mild, humble, charitable, loving, chaste, and zealous this day. I pray that I will not sin this day in any way but especially in those sins that I have often committed (*here name any sin with which you struggle*) and which I firmly resolve to avoid this day, with the help of your grace.

Petition God for the necessary grace to witness to the kingdom.

My Lord and my God, you know my poverty and my weakness. You know that I am unable to do anything good without you. Grant me the necessary grace and the strength to do good this day and to avoid evil. Enable me to patiently witness to your kingdom and to live in your love.

Ask for the prayers of the Blessed Virgin Mary, your guardian angel, and your patron saint.

Holy Virgin Mary, Mother of my Lord, I place myself under your protection this day. I throw myself with confidence into your loving arms. Be this day for me, O Mother of Mercy, my refuge in distress, my consolation in suffering, and my advocate with your Son.

Angel of God, my guardian dear, to whom God's love commits me here, ever this day be at my side, to light, to guard, to rule, and to guide.

O great saint whose name I bear, protect me, pray for me, that like you I may serve God faithfully on earth and one day glorify God forever in heaven.

Read and quietly reflect on the assigned readings from the Word of God and the appropriate reflection provided for this day. Reflections for the season of Advent by Saint Alphonsus Liguori may be found in Section Six, number 2. Reflections for the season of Christmas, also by Saint Alphonsus, may be found in Section Eleven, number 2.

2. Traditional Evening Prayer

In the name of the Father, and of the Son, and of the Holy Spirit. Amen. Come, Holy Spirit, fill the hearts of your faithful people, and enkindle in them the fire of your love.

Place yourself in the presence of God and humbly adore God.

O my God, I present myself to you at the conclusion of another day, to renew the homage of my heart. I praise and worship you, my Creator, my Redeemer, and my Judge. I believe in you because you are the fullness of truth. I hope in you because you are faithful to your promises. I love you with my whole heart because you are infinitely worthy of being loved, and for your sake I love my neighbor as myself.

Give thanks to God for all that God has gifted you with this day.

Enable me, O God, to thank you and praise you for all that you have given me, especially those gifts that I take so often for granted.

You have thought of me and have loved me from all eternity; you have formed me out of nothing; you have redeemed me through the Passion, death, and Resurrection of Jesus; you have made me a member of your Holy Church; you have preserved me from falling into sin. What return, O God, can I make for all of your blessings? O saints and angels, unite with me in praising the God of mercies.

Ask for the necessary grace to recognize any sins that may have been committed this day and for the grace of forgiveness.

O my God, you do not desire the death of the sinner, but rather the conversion of mind and heart. Enlighten my mind so that I may know the sins that I may have committed this day in thought, word, or action. Grant me also the necessary grace of contrition.

At this time, you may find it helpful to examine your conscience. As an aid to this examination, you may choose to use the examination provided in Section Three, number 3, "Advent Reconciliation Service." If you prefer, a more traditional and substantial examination may be found in Section Five, number 9, "Traditional Examination of Conscience." After your examination is complete, you may wish to pray the following prayer or some other expression of sorrow and contrition.

O my God, I heartily repent and am grieved that I have offended you, because you are infinitely good and sin is displeasing to you. I humbly ask you to gift me with your mercy and pardon, through the infinite merits of Jesus Christ. I resolve, with the help of your grace, to do penance for my sins and I will endeavor never more to offend you.

CLOSING PRAYER

O Jesus my savior, grant me your blessing, deliver me from everlasting death, assist your Holy Church, grant peace to all nations, and deliver the holy souls in purgatory. Amen. May the Lord grant me a restful night and a peaceful death.

3. Contemporary Morning Prayer

LITURGY OF THE HOURS

V. O Lord, open my lips.

R. And with my mouth I will proclaim your praise.

V. Glory to the Father, the Son, and the Holy Spirit,

R. Both now and forever. Amen.

Antiphon: I will praise your name forever, Lord (Ps 145:1–7).
    I will extol you, my God and King,
        and bless your name forever and ever.
    Every day I will bless you,
        and praise your name forever and ever.

    Great is the LORD, and greatly to be praised;
        his greatness is unsearchable.

    One generation shall laud your
        works to another,
        and shall declare your mighty acts.
    On the glorious splendor of your majesty,
        and on your wondrous works,
        I will meditate.

    The might of your awesome deeds
        shall be proclaimed,
        and I will declare your greatness.
    They shall celebrate the fame of
        your abundant goodness,
        and shall sing aloud of
        your righteousness.

Glory to the Father, the Son, and the Holy Spirit,
both now and forever. Amen.

Antiphon: *I will praise your name forever, Lord.*

Breath of the Gospel

The breath of the Gospel is a simple form of praying with Scripture. Choose a short passage of Scripture from among those given on page 15, or use a personal favorite from your own copy of Scripture. Read the passage slowly and silently, pausing after phrases and words, allowing the Holy Spirit to lead you in prayer.

Silent Reflection

Canticle of Zechariah *(Lk 1:68–79)*

Blessed be the Lord God of Israel,
    for he has looked favorably on
    his people and redeemed them.
He has raised up almighty savior for us
    in the house of his servant David,
as he spoke through the mouth of
    his holy prophets from of old,
        that we would be saved from our enemies
        and from the hand of all that hate us.
Thus he has shown the mercy
    promised to our ancestors,
    and has remembered his holy covenant,
the oath that he swore to our ancestor Abraham,
    to grant us that we, being rescued
    from the hands of our enemies,
might serve him without fear,
    in holiness and righteousness
    before him all our days.

And you, child, will be called
    the prophet of the Most High;
    for you will go before the Lord
    to prepare his ways,
to give knowledge of salvation to his people
    by the forgiveness of their sins.
By the tender mercy of our God,
    the dawn from on high will break upon us,
    to give light to those who sit in darkness
    and in the shadow of death,
    to guide our feet into the way of peace.

Glory to the Father, the Son, and the Holy Spirit, both now and forever. Amen.

Prayers of Intercession

For Advent, use the following response for each prayer of intercession: O Come, O Come Emmanuel, and hear the prayer I offer for those who are in need.

For Christmas, use the following response for each prayer of intercession: Glory to God in the Highest, and peace to men and women of good will!

Lord, I pray for the Church. May it always be faithful to the Gospel.

Lord, remember those who are without shelter, food, and meaningful employment.

Lord, keep all those I love in your loving care this day.

At this time, please add your own prayers of intercession.

Our Father

Our Father, who art in heaven, holy be your name. Your kingdom come, your will be done, on earth as it is in heaven. Give us this day our daily bread, and forgive us our sins, as we forgive those who sin against us. Lead us not into temptation but deliver us from the evil one. For yours is the Kingdom, the power, and the glory, now and forever. Amen.

Closing Prayer

Almighty God, you have brought us to another day. We give you praise and glory. Fill our hearts with love for you, increase our faith, and in your mercy protect us through this day. We ask this through our Lord Jesus Christ, your Son, who lives and reigns with you and the Holy Spirit, one God, forever and ever. Amen.

4. Contemporary Evening Prayer

LITURGY OF THE HOURS

V. O Lord, open my lips.

R. And with my mouth I will proclaim your praise.

V. Glory to the Father, the Son, and the Holy Spirit,

R. Both now and forever. Amen.

Antiphon for Advent

In the presence of the angels I will sing to you my God (Ps 138:1).

Antiphon for Christmas

Hark! The Herald Angels sing, glory to our newborn King.

I give you thanks, O Lord, with my whole heart;
before the gods I sing your praise.

I bow down toward your holy temple

and give thanks to your name for your steadfast love
    and your faithfulness;
for you have exalted your name and your word
    above everything.

On the day I called, you answered me,
    you increased my strength of soul.

Glory to the Father, the Son, and the Holy Spirit,
both now and forever. Amen.

Antiphon

Repeat the appropriate seasonal antiphon.

Breath of the Gospel

The breath of the Gospel is a simple form of praying with Scripture. Choose a short passage of Scripture from among those given on page 15, or use a personal favorite from your own copy of Scripture. Read the passage slowly and silently, pausing after phrases and words, allowing the Holy Spirit to lead you in prayer.

Silent Reflection

Canticle of Mary *(Lk 1:46–55)*

My soul magnifies the Lord,
    and my spirit rejoices in
    God my Savior,
for he has looked with favor on the
    lowliness of his servant.
Surely, from now on
    all generations will call me blessed;
for the Mighty One has done great things for me,
    and holy is his name.
His mercy is for those who fear him
    from generation to generation.

He has shown strength with his arm;
    he has scattered the proud
    in the thoughts of their hearts.
He has brought down the powerful
    from their thrones,
    and lifted up the lowly;
he has filled the hungry
    with good things,
    and sent the rich away empty.
He has helped his servant Israel,
    in remembrance of his mercy,
according to the promise he made
    to our ancestors,
    to Abraham and to
    his descendants forever.
Glory to the Father, the Son, and the Holy Spirit,
    both now and forever. Amen.

Prayers of Intercession

Lord, I thank you for all the blessings of this day.

Lord, grant your blessings this evening to all those who are in need.

Lord, surround me with your protection this evening and grant that I may have a peaceful night.

At this time, please add your own prayers of intercession.

Our Father

Our Father, who art in heaven, holy be your name. Your kingdom come, your will be done, on earth as it is in heaven. Give us this day our daily bread, and forgive us our sins, as we forgive those who sin against us. Lead us not into temptation but deliver us from the evil one. For yours is the Kingdom, the power, and the glory, now and forever, Amen.

Closing Prayer

Lord, may our evening prayers find favor in your sight. Help us to live our lives according to the teachings of the Gospel. May we follow in the footsteps of your Son, Jesus Christ our Lord, who lives and reigns with you and the Holy Spirit, one God forever and ever. Amen.

Breath of the Gospel

Use any of the following passages where noted in preceding prayer liturgies.

John 7:37–38

On the last day of the festival, the great day, while Jesus was standing there, he cried out, "Let anyone who is thirsty come to me, and let the one who believes in me drink. As the scripture has said, 'Out of the believer's heart shall flow rivers of living water.'"

Philippians 2:10–11

At the name of Jesus every knee should bend, in heaven and on earth and under the earth, and every tongue should confess that Jesus Christ is Lord, to the glory of God the Father.

John 10:14

I am the good shepherd. I know my own and my own know me.

Matthew 25:34

Then the king will say to those at his right hand, "Come, you that are blessed by my Father, inherit the kingdom prepared for you from the foundation of the world."

Matthew 11:28–30

Come to me, all you that are weary and are carrying heavy burdens, and I will give you rest. Take my yoke upon you, and learn from me; for I am gentle and humble in heart, and you will find rest for your souls. For my yoke is easy, and my burden is light.

Matthew 8:23–27

And when he got into the boat, his disciples followed him. A windstorm arose on the sea, so great that the boat was being swamped by the waves; but he was asleep. And they went and woke him up, saying, "Lord, save us! We are perishing!" And he said to them, "Why are you afraid, you of little faith?" Then he got up and rebuked the winds and the sea; and there was a dead calm. They were amazed, saying, "What sort of man is this, that even the winds and the sea obey him?"

John 13:34

I give you a new commandment, that you love one another. Just as I have loved you, you also should love one another.

John 16:13

When the Spirit of truth comes, he will guide you into all the truth; for he will not speak on his own, but will speak whatever he hears, and he will declare to you the things that are to come.

SEASONAL SCRIPTURE PASSAGES

The following Scripture passages have been chosen as appropriate for the season of Advent and Christmas. The passages noted are selections from the assigned gospels for the eight days proceeding the feast of Christmas and for the eight days following. For a complete listing of the liturgical readings of the seasons of Advent and Christmas, refer to the appropriate contemporary meditations in Section Six, number 1, and Section Eleven, number 1.

Scripture Passages for Advent

Mt 1:16	Lk 1:30	Lk 1:42	Lk 1:66
Mt 1:23	Lk 1:31	Lk 1:46	Lk 1:78

Scripture Passages for Christmas

Lk 2:29–32	Mt 2:18	Lk 2:40	Lk 2:19
Jn 1:1	Lk 2:35	Jn 1:3	Mt 2:1

SECTION TWO

The Season of Advent

1. The Meaning of Advent

Advent in the Latin root word is *adventus*, which means coming. Advent is a liturgical season and a time of waiting and expectation, approximately four weeks in length, in preparation for the feast of Christmas. In the Latin Church (commonly known as the Roman Catholic Tradition), the season of Advent begins on the Sunday closest to the feast of the apostle Andrew (November 30) and is considered the beginning of the liturgical year.

The season of Advent may begin as early as November 27, providing for a period of twenty-eight days of preparation, or as late as December 3, providing for a period of twenty-one days.

Advent is closely related to Christmas and cannot be considered apart from that feast. For example, it was not until the birthday of Jesus was universally celebrated on December 25 throughout Christianity that Advent even came into existence. For another, the name itself comes from the ancient names associated with the feast. Adventus, Epiphania, and Natale are all synonymous for the Incarnation and also for the feast that celebrates the historical fact that the Word of God became flesh (human). Understood in this sense, the season of Advent is much more than a preparation period for a historical event; it is rather best understood as a period of celebration and preparation for the coming of God as an event of salvation.

For most Catholics, Advent is considered a time of spiritual preparation for Christmas. The emphasis during Advent is often captured in a phrase that, at first glance, might not seem to have anything to do with Advent. "Remember to keep Christ in Christmas," an obvious reference to the commercial aspect of the days proceeding Christmas day which are counted off as "so many shopping days till Christmas." Advent is often cast as the spiritual tonic for the secular emphasis of the season.

Because of the compressed time period and the fact that, at least in the United States, Advent is the time between two official civil holidays (Thanksgiving Day and Christmas), a festive mood seems to be prevalent. Unfortunately, many people have lost the spirit of the season and are unaware of the primary intent of this period of waiting. Perhaps because of a common pastoral emphasis, many consider the Advent season to be simply a time appropriate for the celebration of the sacrament of reconciliation, and have lost the ascetical significance of the season. Most parishes, recognizing the popular understanding, offer opportunities for the private and the communal celebration of this sacrament during Advent.

Nonetheless, the season of Advent is rich in spiritual traditions and practices and can be an important opportunity for growth and development.

2. Short History of Advent

A short review of the history of the season may serve as an illustration of the rich spiritual potential of the Advent season. The remote beginning of the season may be discovered in the traditions and practices of the Church in France in the early centuries. It was the French custom to have a time of preparation, not for the feast of Christmas but rather for the feast of the Epiphany, which was a baptismal feast in France as well as in different territories of the Christian West. Since the great feast of baptism, Easter, had a period of preparation, it was assumed that this secondary baptismal feast also needed an equal time in preparation. This time of preparation took the form of fasting and prayer, at first for a period of three weeks, but eventually it was expanded to forty days in obvious imitation of the season of Lent. As a result of the relationship, at least in the minds of the people of the time, this period of preparation was called "Saint Martin's Lent," since it commenced on the feast of Saint Martin, November 11.

In A.D. 330, the Council of Saragossa ordered a period of prayer and fasting before the feast of the Epiphany. By 581, the Council of Macon extended this custom to all the dioceses of France, and during the next two hundred years it also became the custom in all the dioceses of England. In each instance, the emphasis was ascetical—a spiritual preparation for the baptismal feast of the Epiphany.

Meanwhile, in Rome, the situation was very different. The Roman Church never celebrated the feast of the Epiphany as a baptismal feast and so never saw a need for an ascetical period of preparation. However, the Roman Church did celebrate Christmas and did have a need for a liturgical season that would precede the celebration of that feast.

Pope Gregory I (590–604) developed the Roman Advent season. He composed prayers, antiphons, and the psalm responses for the season. He also arranged the lectionary and the Divine Office. As a result of his efforts, by the time the Roman Rite was introduced in France, Gregory's Advent was a well-established liturgical season of four weeks. The French Church accepted the Gregorian improvements and added an emphasis on the Second Coming of Our Lord in power and majesty as a central theme. By the time the Advent liturgy worked itself back to Rome, the themes of Advent that we know today were well developed.

3. Advent's Central Emphasis of Preparation

"Prepare the way of the Lord" (Mk 1:3) is the cry of the last great prophet of the Old Testament, John the Baptist; and it is a central theme of Advent. From the First Sunday of Advent and also throughout the season, the two great preparation themes of the Advent season emerge and are dramatically pronounced.

The first theme, Advent as preparation for the first coming of Jesus Christ into the world as man, is obvious. Even the casual participant or observer of Christian ritual and practice would recognize the connection between Advent and the feast of Christmas. The second great

Advent theme, preparation for the Second Coming of Christ at the end of time, is not so obvious. To experience this emphasis, since there is no obvious connection between Christmas and Christ's Second Coming, it would be necessary to actively join in and participate in the rituals of the season, since this theme is made apparent in the liturgical readings of the season.

However, these two themes are theologically connected and essential for an understanding of salvation history, even though they do not necessarily complement each other in practice nor in the popular imagination. At the same time, both themes do celebrate a central idea that is crucial to the Christian expression of faith and belief, the concept of the "already and the not yet." We are already saved, Jesus has already come, the kingdom has already been established; however, at the same time, we are not yet completely saved. Jesus will come again for a second time, and the kingdom has not yet been perfectly experienced by all of God's people. This dynamic of the "already and the not yet" is clearly at work in the Advent season.

Another way of looking at the dynamic of the "already and not yet" is to see it as liturgical, celebrating the "already" of the season, the historical birth of Jesus, and the ascetical, the "not yet," which demands vigilance, preparation, penance, and patience.

4. Advent Understood As a Journey

A proper understanding of the concept of Advent as journey also contains the elements and tension of the "already" and the "not yet."

The liturgical journey of the season situates the season of Advent at the beginning of the Church year. Advent is the starting point for the liturgical designations of the Scripture readings that are proper for the year, the feasts that will be celebrated, and the prayers that will be offered. The liturgical calendar that begins with the First Sunday of Advent will continue to the last Sunday of the Church year, the feast of Christ the King. The calendar marks our journey in cel-ebration of the life and ministry of the Lord from his coming among us as man through his triumphant return to the "right hand of the Father."

The ascetical journey of the season is a spiritual journey in prepa-ration for an event, the birth of the Messiah, and in anticipation of an event that is yet to come, the Second Coming of the Lord in glory and in power. That which marks this ascetical journey is not the feasts and memorials of the liturgical calendar, but rather the ascetical disciplines of prayer, fasting, and vigilance as we wait.

The ascetical journey is also a spiritual remembering of the time our ancestors spent in waiting and in preparation for the "word of God that was to be made flesh." Our maranatha, our "come Lord, Jesus," captures the spirit of those who have gone before us in faith. The penitential practices and the proclamation of the Word of God clearly proclaimed in the assigned Scripture readings for Sundays and weekdays all help us to recall the centuries of longing for the coming of the Messiah, the conception of John the Baptist, and the family history of Mary and Joseph. The writings of the prophet Isaiah are featured during Advent because they so eloquently speak of Israel's longing for salvation.

5. Traditional Hymns of Advent

It is in the traditional hymns of Advent, songs reserved for this spe-cial season of the year, that the themes and the feelings of the Ad-vent season become spoken. The hymns of Advent clearly symbolize the unique emphasis of the season and capture the spirit of waiting and watching.

Two traditional hymns, the ninth century *"Veni, Veni Emmanuel,"* today popularly known as "Come, O Come, Emmanuel," and a hymn from Charles Wesley (1707–1788), "Come, O Long Expected Jesus," are excellent examples.

O come, O come, Emmanuel
And ransom captive Israel,
That mourns in lonely exile here
Until the Son of God appear.
Rejoice! Rejoice! Emmanuel
Shall come to you, O Israel.

Come, O Long Expected Jesus
Born to set your people free;
From our fears and sins release us,
Free us from captivity.

A modern hymn, "Prepare the Way of the Lord" from the Taizé community in France is based on the Gospel of Luke, found in 3:4, 6. This hymn clearly illustrates the twin themes of Advent. The sentiments and the feelings expressed are not limited to a time and a place in the distant past, but are also interpreted as a future event as well.

Prepare the Way of the Lord.
Prepare the way of the Lord,
And all people will see the salvation of our God.

6. Symbols of Advent

The season of Advent features special signs and symbols that have been traditionally reserved for this liturgical season. The symbols of Advent are the creations of believing Christians who have prepared for and celebrated the birth of Christ over the ages. Some are immediately recognizable and others seem to be more modern and perhaps not universally recognized or established in the liturgical expression of the local church.

The most obvious symbol and the most prominent is the Advent wreath. In addition to the Advent wreath, there are other signs and symbols easily recognizable, such as the Jesse tree and the giving tree.

THE ADVENT WREATH

One of the most common symbols used during Advent is the Advent wreath, usually made of evergreen branches formed into a circle. It holds four candles: three purple (or dark blue) and one pink. The three purple candles symbolize the time of preparation, and are lit at the beginning of the first, second, and fourth Sundays of Advent. The pink candle, lit at the beginning of the third week of Advent, is the Church's way of giving us a break. There is a similar Sunday in Lent. Both of these days, within penitential seasons, focus on rejoicing. It is the Church's way of lifting people up within a serious time of repentance and penance to remind them that Jesus' death and Resurrection have won the battle. The first word of the liturgy on these occasions (Gaudete Sunday and Laetare Sunday) is "Rejoice."

The Advent wreath is lit in church at the beginning of each of the Sunday Masses on the four Sundays of Advent. Each week one more candle is lit and prayers are said to correspond to the liturgical theme of the week.

Many families make a small Advent wreath for use at home. Although the candles on the wreath in church are lit only on Sundays, the candles on the family's wreath usually are lit each night of the week, accompanied with a variety of prayers or rituals. Some families place a white or light-colored candle in the middle of the Advent wreath on Christmas Eve to symbolize the coming of the Christ Child. This candle symbolizes the connection between the Old and the New Testaments. Whatever is chosen, prayers and rituals should be appropriate and relevant to all members of the family.

THE JESSE TREE

The Jesse tree receives its name from Jesse, the father of King David, from whose house the lineage of Jesus can be traced through his earthly father, Joseph. The Gospels of Matthew and Luke contain lists of the ancestors of Jesus. Matthew 1:1–17 traces Jesus' lineage back to Abraham, and Luke 3:23–38 links Jesus to Adam. Not every ancestor is mentioned, of course, because the primary purpose is to connect Jesus to Abraham and to Adam. Primarily, this history puts Christians in touch with the continuous longing of the chosen people for a Messiah. Over the days of Advent, the names of significant persons in the Old Testament and quotations from the Old Testament are hung on the branches of the Jesse tree as a preparation for Christmas.

The Jesse tree may be constructed from a small branch of a real tree, anchored in florist's foam, or from pieces of felt cut into the shape of a tree, then glued to a cloth background, or from a large piece of construction paper. The symbols can be constructed in many different ways. Some are drawn or cut and still others are purchased. Popular symbols include representations of Adam, Noah, Abraham, Moses, King David, King Solomon, and, of course, Saint Joseph and the Blessed Mother. A partial listing of the possible names and symbols that can be used on a Jesse tree include:

Name	**Popular Symbol Used**
King David	Crown
Adam	Apple
Jonah	Whale
Noah	Ark or a boat
Jacob	Ladder
Moses	Tablet of the Ten Commandments
Joseph	Colorful coat
Blessed Mother Mary	Rose
Ruth	Sheaf of wheat
Holy Spirit	Dove or flame

ADVENT HOUSE

A popular custom, especially among young children, is the Advent or Christmas house, which is often purchased in a religious goods store. The house features small windows, one of which is opened each day revealing a picture or activity that points to the coming of Jesus. On December 24, the last window is opened, revealing the Nativity scene.

THE GIVING TREE

The giving tree is a variation of the Jesse tree. Church communities sponsor a tree decorated with tags indicating gifts for children in need at Christmas. Clothing sizes and ages are connected with the requests on the tree so that the person taking the tag can easily get the needed item and return the gift to the parish church by a designated date. The gifts are then distributed to the children before Christmas. The giving tree is intended to unite believing Christians in the great message of Jesus "What you do to the least of these, you do to me" (see Mt 25:40).

THE MANGER

An Advent tradition that many families use as a way to actively join in the preparation and anticipation for the feast of Christmas is having children prepare the manger for the family's Nativity scene. Each night, before the children go to bed, the family gathers in front of the manger, and the children are invited to place one piece of straw in the manger for each good deed that they have performed that day. In some families, the opportunity to remove a piece of straw for each deed that was not Christlike is also provided.

ADVENT LITURGICAL COLORS

The traditional liturgical color for the season of Advent is purple or violet. However, it has become the practice in some local churches to substitute a dark blue as the color of choice. The purpose for the emphasis on the dark blue is to emphasize that Advent has a distinctive theme and spiritual emphasis and is not to be considered a "little Lent."

Traditionally, on the Third Sunday of Advent rose-colored vestments are used. This rose color is symbolic of the Christmas joy announced in the first word of the entrance antiphon: "Rejoice," or in Latin, *Gaudete*. For this reason, the Third Sunday of Advent is often called "Gaudete Sunday."

7. The O Antiphons

An antiphon is a song, prayer, or psalm chanted in responsorial fashion. The O Antiphons of Advent share this specific designation and identification but seem to have a special place. Proclaimed for seven days before the vigil of Christmas, they have been popular since the seventh century, achieving their highest popularity during the Middle Ages.

During the Advent season, the closer the feast of Christmas approaches, the more the liturgy accentuates the call to the Savior to "Come!" (*Veni*). During the praying of the Liturgy of the Hours, the official prayer of the church or the "Office" as it is commonly known, the O Antiphons are proclaimed at the praying of the *Magnificat*, near the end of the Hour. Traditionally, the O Antiphons are intoned by a succession of dignitaries in the monastery or the cathedral, beginning with the abbot or rector.

The seven O Antiphons of Advent summarize the hopes of the people in the Old Testament who waited for the coming of the Messiah: O Wisdom, O Lord of Might, O Flower of Jesse's Stem, O Key of David, O Dayspring, O Desire of Nations, and O Emmanuel (God-with-us). The message of the seven antiphons is outlined in the following explanations:

O come, O Wisdom:... Chapter 24 of the Book of Sirach speaks of Wisdom as coming from God and foreshadowing the Divine Word who is Jesus.

O come, O Lord of Might: ... The Messiah would be a powerful Lord. In previous times, this powerful Lord was hidden but now his power and his person will be seen clearly.

O come, O Flower of Jesse's Stem: ... This refers to Jesus' relationship to David. Joseph, Jesus' earthly father, was a descendent of the line of David.

O come, O Key of David: ... David and his descendants (Joseph and Jesus) would hold the key that would unlock heaven.

O come, O Dayspring: ... The Messiah will be like the dawn bringing the hope of a new day. Even death will not stand in his way.

O come, O Desire of Nations: ... The Messiah will not be a Savior just for the house of Israel, but all nations will be ruled by this Prince of Peace.

O come, O Emmanuel: ... Emmanuel means "God-with-us" and is a term that is applied to Jesus in the gospel (Mt 1:23).

Each of the O Antiphons is structured to contain three elements: an invocation to the Messiah under a title inspired principally by the Hebrew Scriptures (Old Testament); an amplification that provides an attribute of the Messiah and further develops the invocation; and, finally, a petition to the coming Savior is linked to the initial invocation. In the paragraphs that follow, each of the O Antiphons is presented using this structure.

O Wisdom, O holy Word of God, you govern all creation with your strong yet tender care. Come and show your people the way to salvation.

Invocation: The coming Christ is personified Wisdom. This is a feature of some biblical writings, especially the Books of Proverbs (1:20; 8:12) and Wisdom (8:14–16). Indeed, he is the Word of God.

The Latin for the phrase "O holy Word of God" is "I came forth from the mouth of the Most High" (see Sir 24:3). That is, he was begotten from the substance of the Father in an eternal generation. "The Lord created me...the first of his acts...when there were no depths I was brought forth" (Prov 8:22–24).

Amplification: The creative and provident activity of this coming Messiah is mentioned: "When he established the heavens, I was there...rejoicing before him always" (Prov 8:27, 30). This conjures up the prologue to John's Gospel: "All things came into being through him" (Jn 1:3). Indeed, he is the creator of the invisible spiritual world as well: "What has come into being in him was life, and the life was the light of all people" (Jn 1:3–4).

Petition: As Wisdom, Christ is the teacher of the way to salvation for all Christians. "I am the way, and the truth, and the life. No one comes to Father except through me" (Jn 14:6). We exhort him to come and teach us that way.

> *O sacred Lord of ancient Israel, who showed yourself to Moses in the burning bush, who gave him the holy law on Sinai mountain: come, stretch out your mighty hand to set us free.*

Invocation: The coming Christ is equated with the Lord of God's people of old. He was the "Covenant of God" (*Adonai*) of the chosen people, who made covenants with Noah, Abraham, Isaac, and Jacob, and with Moses.

Amplification: Amid the many appearances of this Lord, who are mentioned. He appeared to Moses in the burning bush to establish his name "I AM WHO AM" (see Ex 3:2ff). He also appeared on Mount

Sinai to give the Law and establish his people (Ex 20:1ff), going before them with "outstretched arm" (see Ex 6:6).

Petition: As Lord, Christ has the power to free his people as he did at the time of the exodus. We ask that he come and stretch out his arm to set us free from evil, sin, and death.

> *O Flower of Jesse's stem, you have been raised up as a sign for all peoples, kings stand silent in your presence, the nations bow down before you. Come, let nothing keep you from coming to our aid.*

Invocation: The coming Christ is the Flower of Jesse's stem, (usually translated as the root of Jesse or the stump of Jesse), raised up as a sign for all people (see Isa 11:1, 10). Recall John's Gospel: "And I, when I am lifted from the earth, will draw all people to myself" (Jn 12:32). Thus, out of the old root of Jesse, a new branch buds forth; the throne of David will again be occupied. "The Lord God will give to him the throne of his ancestor David. He will reign over the house of Jacob forever" (Lk 1:32–33).

Amplification: Lifted up from the earth through his death on the cross (see Jn 12:32–33), the coming Christ will conquer hearts. He will enjoy such glory that even kings will stand dumbstruck in wonder and awe (see Isa 52:15). All the earth will assemble and acknowledge him as Lord and Ruler (see Isa 60:1–3).

Petition: However, we know that Christ is not yet fully ruler of all hearts—beginning with our own. We ask that he come to be the sign, not only for the world but for our own souls.

> *O Key of David, O royal power of Israel, controlling at your will the gate of heaven: come, break down the prison walls of death for those who dwell in darkness and the shadow of death, and lead your captive people into freedom.*

Invocation: The coming Christ is the key of David (see Isa 22:22 and Rev 3:7) and the royal power of Israel. The six-pointed star is the Jewish symbol for the shield, or key of David. It was a symbol of God and his holy name. At the same time, it was a sign of the promised Messiah (star of Balaam: "a star shall come out of Jacob" [Num 24:17]). The words "royal power" translate a word that means literally "scepter," denoting power over God's people.

Amplification: Christ is the royal Messiah "who opens and no one will shut, who shuts and no one opens" (Rev 3:7). He had the keys to the heavenly city of David (see Isa 22:22), the new Jerusalem over which God has supreme authority. Thus, he is the chief steward of the blessings of salvation: "All authority in heaven and on earth has been given to me" (Mt 28:18). In turn, Jesus has entrusted his power to the Church through its head, Peter: "I will give you the keys of the kingdom of heaven" (Mt 16:19).

Petition: In a more extended petition than the others, we ask that Christ may use his key to unlock the prison of sin ("darkness and death") to which all human beings are subject. More specifically, we ask that he may free us from the prison of selfish attachments to which all of us are prone.

> *O Radiant Dawn, splendor of eternal light, sun of justice; come, shine on those who dwell in darkness and the shadow of death.*

Invocation: The coming Christ is the Radiant Dawn, or "Daybreak on High." This title stems from the Septuagint (Old Testament, Greek translation) rendering of the Hebrew word for "scion, branch," a messianic title used in three places (Jer 23:5; Zech 3:8 and Zech 6:12). It is also used daily in the Canticle of Zechariah at Morning Prayer in which the aged priest alludes to the "Dayspring on high" who will come to visit his people.

Amplification: This Christ is the "splendor of eternal light" or "the reflection of God's glory" (Heb 1:3). Thus, it is an apt phrase to indicate the eternal and consubstantial origin of the Son from the Father. At the same time, Christ is also the "Sun of Righteousness" mentioned in Malachi 4:2, another messianic title. What the sun does for the sphere of nature, Christ does for the kingdom of God. He emits rays of holiness and grace.

Petition: We ask this "Sun of Justice" to come and shine on those who are dwelling "in darkness and in the shadow of death" (Lk 1:79). These dwellers in darkness are both those who do not know Christ and those who do—for even in the latter there is much darkness.

> *O King of all the nations, the only joy of every human heart, O Keystone of the mighty arch of humanity, come and save the creatures you fashioned from the dust.*

Invocation: The coming Christ is the king of all the nations (see Jer 10:7) and the "only joy of every human heart" (Hag 2:7, Vulgate text). Thus, he is the one eagerly and explicitly awaited by the Israelites; but just as eagerly awaited by all the nations.

Amplification: This Christ is also the keystone or cornerstone promised by God (see Isa 28:16); the foundation, spiritual support, and mainstay of the Church (see Mt 21:42). He is the mighty arch of all, uniting Jew and Gentile. "There is no longer Jew or Greek, there is no longer slave or free, there is no longer male and female; for all of you are one in Christ Jesus" (Gal 3:28).

Petition: We ask Christ the Keystone to come and save the creatures that he fashioned (see Gen 2:7). Without Christ, there is no hope for salvation. May his coming now in mystery lead to the salvation of all that yearn for him, whether they know it or not.

O Emmanuel, king and lawgiver, desire of all nations, Savior of all people, come and set us free, Lord our God.

Invocation: This coming Christ is not only the Messiah, the Lord, the Ruler of all. He is also Emmanuel, that is, God-with-us (see Isa 7:14; 8:8, 10). God has become one of us in all things except sin so we may become like him.

Amplification: This Christ is our King and lawgiver (see Isa 33:22). He will accomplish for us not only what human kings and lawgivers do for their people but much more. For he is the "Expectation of the nations": the scepter will not pass from Judah, nor a rule from his thigh, till he is sent. He is also their Savior. "The Father has sent his Son as the Savior of the World" (1 Jn 4:14).

Petition: We ask Emmanuel to come and set us free from sin and death, for he is our Lord and our God (see Jn 20:28).

8. Liturgical Readings of Advent

The liturgical readings for Advent are carefully planned. The Sunday themes move from the Second Coming of Christ on the First Sunday of Advent to John the Baptist preparing for the coming of Jesus on the second and third Sundays. The fourth Sunday, the Gospel of Matthew or Luke, announces the conception of Jesus and Mary's visit to her cousin, Elizabeth, John the Baptist's mother. During the first nine week-days of Advent, the first reading for the eucharistic liturgy comes from the Book of Isaiah. These readings express the compassion of God for his people and the longing of the people for the messianic age.

After the Thursday of the second week of Advent, the gospel readings speak of John the Baptist, while the first readings are either from Isaiah or a reading compatible with the gospel. From December 17 to December 24, the readings are taken from Matthew and Luke. These present the events that lead up to the birth of Jesus.

Many families and individuals find it helpful to read parts of these Scriptures each day of Advent. The readings put us in touch with the centuries of longing on the part of the Old Testament saints like David, Solomon, Isaiah, Jeremiah, and all those whose names we will never know. This is the unbroken tradition of those who prayed and waited for the faithful God to bless his people with a Messiah.

A listing of the Advent liturgical readings for each day may be found in Section Six, pages 104–124. The readings include a suggested meditative reflection for each day of the Advent season.

SECTION THREE

Traditional Practices of Advent

1. Advent Scripture Service

The theme of the service that follows is to make ready the way of the Lord. This service is intended for congregational use but may be easily adapted for private prayer and reflection.

Celebrant: Let us raise our hearts to the Lord. No one who hopes in the Lord will be disappointed.

All: We place our trust in you, O Lord, for our salvation belongs to you alone.

Celebrant: Lord Jesus Christ, Savior of the world. You are present with us as our God and our Redeemer. The expectation of the Old Testament, the longing of your people for the coming of God and our redemption, finds fulfillment in you.

All: Come, Lord Jesus.

READING OF THE WORD

Isaiah 7:10–15, followed by a period of silent reflection.

Response to the Word of God

Celebrant: For thousands of years humanity looked for your coming. At the dawn of human history, when our first parents sinned, your coming was promised, for God said to the serpent:

All: "I will put enmity between you and the woman, between your seed and her seed; he shall crush your head."

Celebrant: Abraham could see your day from afar; all nations of the earth would be blessed in one of his descendants.

All: In you, O Lord; for you chose to become a man, a son of Abraham.

Celebrant: A thousand years before your coming the promise was made to David, Israel's great king, that his line would never perish; that his Son would rule over all the people of the world.

All: You, Lord, are the Son of David, the King of the new Israel, of redeemed humanity. You are our King forever.

Celebrant: In ancient times, the prophets announced your coming to the people. The picture they drew became ever clearer: Son of the virgin, friend of the poor and oppressed, Redeemer from our sins, man of sorrows, judge of the world, strong God! From generation to generation humankind waited and hoped.

All: But now you are with us. The first coming is now a reality. You have come and redeemed the world.

SECOND READING

Mark 1:3–8, followed by a period of silent reflection.

RESPONSE TO THE WORD OF GOD

Celebrant: Lord Jesus Christ, incarnate Son of God. You are present here among us in the holy Eucharist.

All: We kneel before you and adore you.

Celebrant: In a few weeks we will celebrate again the great feast of your birth, the remembrance of your first coming to this earth. Make our hearts ready for these holy days, so that we may receive the overflowing fullness of that grace you merited for us by your Incarnation. Sink the earnest words of the Baptist deep into our hearts: "Make ready the way of the Lord! Make straight his path."

All: Give your blessing, Lord, to our prayers and our penance during this holy season of Advent.

Celebrant: Lead us to true conversion and improvement in our lives on the holy feast of Christmas, so that we may once again experience the salvation that God has prepared for us in you, our Lord and our Redeemer.

All: Give us the grace to know you, the incarnate Son of God, ever more profoundly and to love you more sincerely.

Celebrant: Let the heavens rejoice.

All: And the earth be glad.

Celebrant: For our God is coming and will show mercy to the poor.

All: He is our savior.

Celebrant: Let us pray. O God, with joyful longing we look forward to the holy feast of Christmas, when we will celebrate once again the human birth of your son.

All: We receive him with joy as our savior.

Celebrant: Give us full sharing in his redemption so that we may raise our faces with confidence when he comes to judge the world, who lives and reigns with you forever and ever.

All: Amen.

Celebrant: Glory to the Father, and to the Son, and to the Holy Spirit.

All: As it was in the beginning, is now, and ever shall be, world without end. Amen.

THIRD READING

Luke 1:26–38, followed by a period of silent reflection.

RESPONSE TO THE WORD OF GOD

Celebrant: Holy Mary, Mother of our Lord. We think also of you in this holy season of Advent. It is your image that stands as the first sign of redemption over the darkness of sin and death that covered all people when Adam and Eve sinned.

All: You are that woman who, in your Son, would win victory over the serpent.

Celebrant: Together with the Redeemer, you also, his mother, were announced to a waiting world through the prophet.

All: "Behold a virgin shall conceive and give birth to a son; his name shall be Emmanuel, God-With-Us."

Celebrant: In your Immaculate Conception, holiest Virgin, the first light of a new day broke forth. You are the dawn that heralded for the world the rising of its true light, who is Christ the Lord! Redeemed by the power of your son, you gave to our world our Redeemer.

All: We praise you for your Immaculate Conception, holy virgin Mary.

Celebrant: With the angels message, the final hour of the great Advent dawned; the waiting of our world for the promised Redeemer found fulfillment. For all humanity you consented to God's plan of salvation. Thus, you became a new Eve, a new mother of all the living, the mother of God's children.

All: We are grateful to you, O holy Virgin, Mother of our Lord, and our mother, too.

CLOSING PRAYER

Celebrant: Let us pray. Our Father in heaven, each year you gladden us with the expectation of the feast of our redemption. Please grant that as we joyfully receive your only begotten son as our savior, we may also one day welcome him confidently as our Judge, Jesus Christ, your Son and our Lord, for he lives and reigns with you in the unity of the Holy Spirit, God forever.

All: Amen.

2. Advent Vesper Service

Most churches celebrate an Advent vesper service, a special liturgy centering on our expectation of Jesus' coming into the midst of humankind as the Light of the World. The vesper prayer is usually celebrated at dusk, as day is turning into night, and proclaims that the darkness of night will not conquer the light of Jesus. The service usually consists of singing the O Antiphons (often with the song "O Come, O Come, Emmanuel"), lighting of the Easter candle and the Advent wreath, and readings of Scripture, primarily those from the prophets proclaiming the coming of the Messiah. Because Christian tradition holds that the ecclesiastical day begins at sunset in accord with Genesis 1:5 ("And there was evening and there was morning, the first day"), "vespers," or the Office of Evening, is the first hour of the new Church day.

An Advent vesper service calls us to embrace the new beginning that is symbolized by Jesus, who is the Light of the World. This imagery is especially appropriate considering the approaching winter solstice. In the beginning of Advent, the nights grow progressively longer, and then right before Christmas, the winter solstice marks the light's reclaiming of the world.

The theme of the following vesper service is expressed thusly: "See!

The ruler of the earth shall come, the Lord who will take from us the heavy burden of our exile." The following service is arranged for congregational use but can easily be adapted and used for private recitation.

LIGHTING OF THE CANDLE

The congregation stands as a lighted candle is brought forth in procession while the following hymn is sung to the tune of "O God, Our Help in Ages Past."

The People That in Darkness Walked

The people that in darkness walked
Have seen a glorious light;
The light has shone on them who dwelt
In death's surrounding night.
To hail you, Sun of Righteousness,
The gath'ring nations come:
Rejoicing as when reapers bear
Their harvest treasures home.
To us a child of hope is born,
To us a son is giv'n;
Him shall the tribes of earth obey,
Him all the hosts of heav'n.
His name shall be the Prince of Peace,
For evermore adored,
The Wonderful, the Counselor,
The great and mighty Lord.

PSALMODY

The congregation is seated. During the singing and recitation of the psalm, incense may be used. The following is from Psalm 141:1–5, 8.

Leader: Lord, may our prayers rise like incense before you.

All: Lord, may our prayers rise like incense before you.

Group I: I call upon you, O Lord; come quickly to me; give ear to my voice when I call to you.

Group II: Let my prayer be counted as incense before you, and the lifting up of my hands as an evening sacrifice.

Group I: Set a guard over my mouth, O Lord; keep watch over the door of my lips. Do not turn my heart to any evil, to busy myself with wicked deeds.

Group II: In company with those who work iniquity, do not let me eat of their delicacies. Let the righteous strike me; let the faithful correct me.

Group I: But my eyes are turned toward you, O God, my Lord; in you I seek refuge; do not leave me defenseless.

All: Glory to the Father, and to the Son, and to the Holy Spirit, as it was in the beginning, is now, and ever shall be, world without end. Amen.

SILENT REFLECTION

The assembly pauses for silent meditation.

ANTIPHON
Psalm 24:1–6

Leader: Welcome Christ the Lord, he is the King of Glory.

All: Welcome Christ the Lord, he is the King of Glory.

Group I: The earth is the Lord's and all that is in it, the world, and those who live in it; for he has founded it on the seas, and established it on the rivers.

Group II: Who shall ascend the hill of the Lord? And who shall stand in his holy place? Those who have clean hands and pure hearts, who do not lift up their souls to what is false, and do not swear deceitfully.

Group I: They will receive blessing from the Lord, and vindication from the God of their salvation. Such is the company of those who seek him, who seek the face of the God of Jacob.

All: Glory to the Father, and to the Son, and to the Holy Spirit, as it was in the beginning, is now, and ever shall be, world without end. Amen.

PSALM PRAYER

Leader: Loving Father, fill us with joy and love as we prepare our hearts for the coming of our Lord and Savior. May our remembrance of his birth inspire us to deeds of love and mercy. We ask this through our Lord Jesus Christ, your Son, who lives and reigns with you and the Holy Spirit, one God, forever and ever.

All: Amen.

READING FROM SCRIPTURE

Suggested readings include Isa 11:1–10, Isa 40:1–5, 9–11, and Bar 5:1–9. Or the following from Isa 7:10–14.

Reader: A reading from the book of the prophet Isaiah.
The Lord spoke to Ahaz, saying, "Ask a sign of the Lord your God; let it be deep as Sheol or high as heaven." But Ahaz said, "I will not ask, and I will not put the Lord to the test." Then Isaiah said: "Hear then, O house of David! Is it too little for you to weary [people], that you weary my God also? Therefore the Lord himself will give you a sign. Look, the young woman is with child and shall bear a son, and shall name him Immanuel." This is the Word of the Lord.

SILENT REFLECTION OR HOMILY

The assembly may silently reflect on the Scripture passage, or the celebrant may preach a homily.

GOSPEL CANTICLE: THE *MAGNIFICAT*

All stand as the Magnificat *is spoken or sung. Incense may be used during the reciting or singing of the canticle.*

ANTIPHON
Luke 1:46–55

Leader: Savior of all people, come and set us free.

All: Savior of all people, come and set us free.

Group I: My soul magnifies the Lord, and my spirit rejoices in God my Savior.

Group II: For he has looked with favor on the lowliness of his servant. Surely, from now on all generations will call me blessed; for the Mighty One has done great things for me, and holy is his name.

Group I: His mercy is for those who fear him from generation to generation. He has shown strength with his arm; he has scattered the proud in the thoughts of their hearts.

Group II: He has brought down the powerful from their thrones, and lifted up the lowly.

Group I: He has filled the hungry with good things, and sent the rich away empty.

Group II: He has helped his servant Israel, in remembrance of his mercy, according to the promise he made to our ancestors, to Abraham, and to his descendants forever. Amen.

All: Glory to the Father, and to the Son, and to the Holy Spirit, as it was in the beginning, is now, and ever shall be, world without end. Amen.

INTERCESSIONS

The assembly stands.

Leader: We long for the coming of Jesus Christ. Let us bring before him our petitions.

Response: Come O Christ, Emmanuel!

Leader: We pray for all those who do not have a voice: the poor, the oppressed of our world, the young who are lonely, the aged sick, and those who suffer alone, we pray.

Response: Come O Christ, Emmanuel!

Leader: Help our community recognize you, O Christ, in the lives of all who pray with us. Open our hearts and hands to offer deeds of mercy and love, we pray.

Response: Come O Christ, Emmanuel!

Leader: Lift up those who are burdened with sadness and depression. Give hope to those who are jobless, shelter to the homeless, and protection for those who travel, we pray.

Response: Come O Christ, Emmanuel!

OUR FATHER

Our Father, who art in heaven, holy be your name. Your kingdom come, your will be done, on earth as it is in heaven. Give us this day our daily bread, and forgive us our sins, as we forgive those who sin against us. Lead us not into temptation but deliver us from the evil one. For yours is the Kingdom, the power, and the glory, now and forever. Amen.

CLOSING

Leader: May almighty God have mercy on us, forgive us our sins, and bring us to life everlasting.

All: Amen.

Leader: Let us go in the peace of Christ.

All: Thanks be to God.

3. Advent Reconciliation Service

Advent has a penitential aspect similar to Lent. Christians, and those from other religious traditions, perform penance to shake free the attachments to sin and the distractions that keep them from recognizing the presence of God in their lives. Sin is often understood as an attempt to place an individual in the center of life, while reconciliation and penance seeks to allow a person to place God in the center.

The Advent Reconciliation Service that follows is arranged for congregational use but may be easily adapted for personal use. Its theme may be expressed in the words of Saint Charles Borromeo: "When we remove all obstacles to God's presence, God will come, at any hour and moment, to dwell spiritually in our hearts, bringing with him the riches of his grace."

CALL TO WORSHIP

The congregation stands as the Church calls on us to understand that Christ, who came once in flesh, is prepared to come again.

SUGGESTED HYMNS

It is most appropriate to begin the service with an Advent hymn. The following suggested hymns are found in most Catholic hymnals. "O Come, O Come Emmanuel," "Creator of the Stars of Night," "On Jordan's Bank," "There's a Wideness in God's Mercy."

GREETING

Leader: We gather to celebrate the sacrament of reconciliation. We pray for openness to confess our sins. May the Lord grant us pardon and peace as we make ourselves ready for the celebration of the Christmas feast.

OPENING PRAYER

Leader: God of mercy and compassion, hear us as we call upon you for mercy. As you have sent your Son, Jesus Christ, into our world as a sign of your merciful love, so now at this moment, send down your mercy and pardon on your people gathered to confess their sins. We ask this through Christ our Lord. Amen.

LITURGY OF THE WORD

The congregation is seated for the following.

FIRST READING
Isaiah 63:17, 64:1

Reader: Why have you made us stray from your ways? Why have you let our heart become hard so that we do not fear you? Return for the sake of your servants, the tribes of your inheritance. Why have the irreligious people invaded your sanctuary? Why have our enemies trampled it down? For too long we have become like those you do not rule, like those who do not bear your name. Oh, that you would rend the heavens and come down! The mountains would quake at your presence. As when fire sets brushwood ablaze and causes water to boil, make the nations know your name, and your enemies tremble. This is the Word of the Lord.

RESPONSORIAL PSALM

Psalm 85:4–7 (note: a sung response may be used instead of the recited psalm).

All: God, you have withdrawn your wrath, and turned from your burning rage.

Group I: Restore us, God our savior;
Put away altogether your indignation.

Group II: Will your anger be ever with us,
Carried over to all generations?
Will you not give us life anew,
That your people may rejoice in you?

Group I: Show us, O Lord, your unfailing love
And grant us your saving help.

All: God, you have withdrawn your wrath, and turned from your burning rage.

SECOND READING
1 Thessalonians 5:14–25

Reader: We urge you to warn the idle, encourage those who feel discouraged, sustain the weak, and have patience with everyone. See that no one repays evil for evil, but try to do good, whether among yourselves or towards others. Rejoice always, pray without ceasing, and give thanks to God at every moment. This is the will of God, your vocation as Christians. Do not quench the Spirit, do not despise the prophets warnings. Put everything to the test and hold fast to what is good. Avoid evil, wherever it may be. May the God of Peace make you holy and bring you to perfection. May you be completely blameless, in spirit, soul and body, till the coming of Christ Jesus, our Lord; he who called you is faithful and will do it. Brothers and sisters pray for us. This is the Word of the Lord.

GOSPEL
Mark 2:13–17

Reader: When Jesus went our again beside the lake, a crowd came to him and he taught them. As he walked along, he saw a tax collector sitting in his office. This was Levi, the son of Alpheus. Jesus said to him, "Follow me." And Levi got up and followed him. And so it happened that while Jesus was eating in Levi's house, tax collectors and sinners were sitting with him and his disciples—for there were indeed many of them. But there were also teachers of the Law of the Pharisees party, among those who followed Jesus, and when they saw him eating with sinners and tax collectors, they said to his disciples, "Why! He eats with tax collectors and sinners!" Jesus heard them and answered, "Healthy people do not need a doctor, but sick people do. I did not come to call the righteous but sinners." The Gospel of the Lord.

HOMILY

A homily or period of reflection is appropriate at this time. The homily should reflect on the readings of the Word of God and prepare the congregation for the examination of conscience that follows.

EXAMINATION OF CONSCIENCE

The congregation kneels or is seated for this portion of the service.

Priest: Let us pray. Lord Jesus, open my mind and heart to your Holy Spirit. Show me where I am failing to love your heavenly Father. Show me where I am failing to love you, failing to accept you as my

Savior, failing to seek you and yield to you as my Lord. Show me where I am failing to love the Holy Spirit, failing to be open and to be led by Wisdom and Love.

First Reader: Let us examine our relationship with God.

Am I faithful to daily prayer?

Am I faithful to Mass?

Do I trust God's loving care for me? How do I show this trust?

Do I make time to read Scripture, that I may know and hear Jesus and his Father?

Am I angry with or afraid of God?

Second Reader: Let us examine our relationships with those nearest to us.

Have I failed to respect any family member or friend?

Have I failed to accept anyone just as he or she is?

Have I been patient with another's differences?

Have I been sensitive to another's needs and weaknesses?

Third Reader: Let us examine our relationships with everyone else.

Do I despise any group of people? If so, why?

Do I discriminate against any group or individual because of race, religion, nationality, politics, age, profession, gender, or any other reason?

Do I consider any group or individual inferior to me? If so, why?

Fourth Reader: Let us examine our relationships with God's other creatures.

Have I spoiled any part of creation? If so, why?

Have I abused animals?

Have I been wasteful?

Am I too fond of money?

Do I act as though everything I have is mine to do with what I like?

Am I openhanded and generous?

Do I drive responsibly and with consideration for others?

Do I make positive contributions to the community? If not, why not?

Fifth Reader: Let us examine our relationships with ourselves.

Do I feel angry often? If so, is it because I expect everything and everyone to march to my beat? Am I acting as though I were God?

Am I seeking to know God's will so I may consent and cooperate?

Am I unwilling or afraid to say, "Yes" to God? If so, why?

Do I cherish and care for my body as the gift of God? If not, why not?

Do I live by the pleasure principle ("I want what I want when I want it") in any area of my life?

Sixth Reader: Let us examine aspects of human freedom.

Am I the prisoner of fear, anxiety, worry, guilt, inferiority, or hatred of myself?

Do I hand over the past to God's merciful love? Or do I allow it to trouble me still?

Do I plan prudently for future things that are within my choice and control and hand the rest to God's wise love?

Do I fret with worry, anticipating what might happen?

RITE OF RECONCILIATION

General Confession of Sins

The congregation stands for this portion of the prayer service.

Priest: Let us pray in the words that Jesus taught us.

All: Our Father, who art in heaven, holy be your name. Your kingdom come, your will be done, on earth as it is in heaven. Give us this day our daily bread, and forgive us our sins, as we forgive those who sin against us. Lead us not into temptation but deliver us from the evil one. For yours is the Kingdom, the power, and the glory, now and forever. Amen.

Priest: Let us pray. Lord, we come before you asking for mercy and the forgiveness of our sins. We confess that we are sinners. Through the ministry of the Church, grant us pardon from all our sins. We give you thankful praise in the name of Jesus, our Lord and Savior.

All: Amen.

RECONCILIATION

At this time, the individual confession of sins, within the celebration of the sacrament of reconciliation, is most appropriate. During this period it is suggested that a hymn, such as "Lord, Have Mercy" or some other hymn asking for mercy and forgiveness, be sung. During this period of individual confession and absolution, it is also suggested that the assembled congregation pray for their brothers and sisters who are celebrating the sacrament and for healing and reconciliation throughout the world.

CONCLUDING RITE

Proclamation of Praise
Psalm 9:1–2

All: I will give thanks to the Lord with my whole heart;
I will tell of all your wonderful deeds.
I will be glad and exult in you;
I will sing praise to your name, O most High.

CONCLUDING PRAYER OF THANKSGIVING

The assembly stands for this portion of the reconciliation service.

Priest: Let us pray. All holy Father, you have shown us your mercy and made us a new creation in the likeness of your Son. Make us living signs of your love for the whole world to see. We ask this through Christ our Lord.

All: Amen.

BLESSING

Priest: May the Lord guide your hearts in the way of his love and fill you with Christlike patience.

All: Amen.

Priest: May he give you strength to walk in newness of life and to please him in all things.

All: Amen.

Priest: May almighty God bless you, in the name of the Father, and of the Son, and of the Holy Spirit.

All: Amen.

Priest: The Lord has freed you from your sins. Go in peace.

All: Thanks be to God.

A psalm or hymn may be sung or the sign of peace given in closing.

4. Blessing of the Advent Wreath

The blessing of the Advent wreath can encourage a wonderful sense of participation in the Advent spiritual journey. It is a wonderful devotion for the family, but it is also an appropriate devotion for those who live a single vocation—the blessing and the daily prayer does not have to be a group activity. In the format that follows, a person should be chosen on the first night to read the blessing and a second person should be chosen (if applicable) to proclaim the Scripture and to read the reflection provided. A third person, after an appropriate period of silence, may read the concluding prayer. For those wishing to add more selections from Scripture, it is appropriate to read the designated psalm response each day from Section Six, Daily Meditations for Advent, on pages 104–124, in place of the Scripture provided below.

For families with younger children and for those who might prefer a more participatory Advent wreath prayer, the family Advent wreath blessing follows this selection.

INTRODUCTORY PRAYER

All: O God, bless our wreath and be with us as we prepare our hearts for the coming of Christ. As we light the candle each day, help us to keep our own hearts burning with your love.

PRAYER FOR WEEK ONE

Preparatory Scripture: "So be on the watch. Pray constantly for the strength to stand secure before the Son of Man" (Lk 21:36).

Reader: In the first week of Advent, we prepare ourselves for the Lord's coming into our world and into our lives. We ask, "In what area of my life do I stand at a distance from God?" We examine our relationships with family, friends, classmates, business associates, and neighbors. Is our faith reflected in each experience of human contact? Is love of God and neighbor the basis for our interaction with others?

At this point, the first Advent candle is lit.

PRAYER

Reader: Almighty and loving God, we have searched our hearts and reviewed our love for your people. Some relationships overflow with love while others have been found wanting. Yet it is our desire that you be a part of every human experience. We beg you now to fill our hearts with your love and sharpen our awareness of your presence in every moment so that wherever we go and whatever we do, we will always stand secure before you. Amen.

PRAYER FOR WEEK TWO

Preparatory Scripture: "Make ready the way of the Lord. Clear him a straight path" (Lk 3:4).

Reader: In the second week of Advent, we consider our relationships with ourselves and with God. We ask, "Do I always appreciate the union of the divine and the human that makes me who I am?" Are we aware of the wonder of "self," the gift bestowed upon us by our Creator? Do we appreciate and use our talents, energies, charms, and abilities for God's glory? In prayer and worship, are we in touch with the divine presence around us?

At this point, the second Advent candle is lit.

PRAYER

Reader: Almighty and loving God, you who dwell within our hearts at every waking moment, keep us always close to you. Help us to recognize and appreciate the gifts and talents you have given us. Teach us to use our energies for the good of others and the glory of your Son, Jesus, whose promise is too precious to ignore. Keep our hearts and minds ever alert to your personal and loving touch in every prayer, in every act of worship. Amen.

PRAYER FOR WEEK THREE

Preparatory Scripture: "He will baptize you in the Holy Spirit and in fire" (Lk 3:16).

Reader: In the third week of Advent, we are called to respond to the gifts and graces we received in our baptism. We ask, "Does my life today fulfill the expectations and responsibilities of bearing the name of Christian?" What are we doing for the hungry, the oppressed, the sick, and the lonely? Do we truly care about the needs of others? Do we accomplish cheerfully all that is expected of us in the workplace or the classroom?

At this point, the third Advent candle is lit.

PRAYER

Reader: Almighty and loving God, your Son has taught us the way to live as your children. We were blessed in our baptisms with special gifts and graces, and still there are times when we find it hard to be all that we should be. We ask for an increased awareness of the needs of others and for the courage to stand up for those who cannot stand up for themselves. Please, God, help us to so live in your grace that all who know us will know you and your love. Amen.

PRAYER FOR WEEK FOUR

Preparatory Scripture: "Blest is she who trusted that the Lord's words to her would be fulfilled" (Lk 1:45).

Reader: In the fourth week of Advent, we consider Mary's trust in God's promise, her joy in his goodness to her. We ask, "Am I ready to receive and celebrate the coming of the Son of God?" We have considered our relationships, our love of God and God's love for us, and we have responded with an awakened concern for the needs of others. Now we may echo Mary's words: "My being proclaims the greatness of the Lord. My spirit finds joy in God my savior."

At this point, the fourth Advent candle is lit.

Reader: Almighty and loving God, soon the whole world will celebrate the birth of your Son, Jesus. Even as we rejoice in our remembrance of his birth at Bethlehem, we find greater comfort in his promise to come again. May our preparations for this wondrous season remain with us, increase in us, and become as much a part of us as our breathing and our heartbeat. Then may we say, "Come, Lord Jesus, we are ready." Amen.

5. Advent Wreath Blessing for the Family

Advent can be a precious time for families to recognize anew Christ's peace within the home and within the heart of each family member. If families truly use the Advent season for reflection, it can be a time for each family member to become closer to God and to one another. The Family Advent Wreath Blessing is intended to help families live the Advent season fully and to celebrate together the wonder of the birth of Jesus. Although the blessing is intended to be celebrated each evening, at the very least it should be celebrated on the appropriate Sundays of the Advent season. The blessing for each of the four weeks of Advent follows.

WEEK ONE

Permit the youngest family member to light the first purple candle.

Parent: Lord, you are the light of our world.

Children: O come, O come, Emmanuel.
This response may be sung if you wish.

Parent: O gracious God of promise, we prepare to worship together as we await the fulfillment of your wondrous plan. Help us to grow as we hear your Word and live in your love.

Children: O come, O come, Emmanuel.

Parent: May the light of your love always shine in our hearts.

Children: Amen.

WEEK TWO

Permit the second youngest family member to light two purple candles for this week.

Parent: Lord, you are the light and hope of our world.

Children: Let it be done to me according to your Word.

Parent: God of the angels and of all humankind, we have placed our hopes in your hands. We say, with Mary, "Let it be done with me according to your Word." Like Mary, we await the joy to come when your Son shall be born in our hearts.

Children: Let it be done to me according to your Word.

Parent: May our faith always be a light to others.

Children: Amen.

WEEK THREE

Permit the third youngest family member to light two purple candles and one pink candle.

Parent: Lord, your light will guide us on our journey.

Children: Keep us always on your holy way.

Parent: O God of the eternal journey, we have kept our feet on your path. Help us never to stray, even when this holy season has ended.

Children: Keep us always on your holy Way.

Parent: Gather our family now into your light.

Children: Amen.

WEEK FOUR

Permit those members of the family who have not yet had a turn to light one of the four candles for this week, or have a parent light them all.

Parent: God, may the light of your Son and this holy season never grow dim.

Children: O come, let us adore him.

Parent: God of Jesus, we thank you for the gift of your Son. Nothing that we receive beneath our tree can compare with the love that prompted you to send your Son into our world.

Children: O come, let us adore him.

Parent: As we celebrate the birth of Jesus, with singing and bright Christmas lights, let us search for ways to keep a song in our hearts and the light of love in our eyes.

Children: Amen.

6. Advent Family Prayers

Each evening of Advent, before the family retires, gather around the dining-room table, the family crèche, or the Advent wreath. Light a candle and designate one member of the family to be the reader for the evening. Only the reader needs the text, all other members of the family will repeat each day of the week the designated antiphon, which can be easily learned.

WEEK ONE
Theme for Week One

"In the sixth month the angel Gabriel was sent by God to a town in Galilee called Nazareth" (Lk 1:26).

Sunday, First Week of Advent

Reader: Lord, send your angels to guide us.

All: Lord, send your angels to guide us.

Reader: Lord God, you chose the angel Gabriel as your special messenger to tell Mary she was to be the mother of God's only Son. We ask you, Lord, to send Gabriel to our family this day. Let us feel the angel's presence guiding us and protecting us.

All: Lord, send your angels to guide us.

Reader: Amen.

Monday, First Week of Advent

Reader: Lord, send your angels to guide us.

All: Lord, send your angels to guide us.

Reader: Lord God, you chose Gabriel to travel the long journey between heaven and earth. Sometimes we feel tired, and we don't want to do anything more. During those times, fill us with the spirit and the energy of the angel Gabriel.

All: Lord, send your angels to guide us.

Reader: Amen.

Tuesday, First Week of Advent

Reader: Lord, send your angels to guide us.

All: Lord, send your angels to guide us.

Reader: Angel Gabriel, your name means the "power of God." In our family, we sometimes need God's power to help us make hard decisions. Lord, send your power to us this day. Let your power stand at the front of our home to protect us.

All: Lord, send your angels to guide us.

Reader: Amen.

Wednesday, First Week of Advent

Reader: Lord, send your angels to guide us.

All: Lord, send your angels to guide us.

Reader: Angel Gabriel, you were one of the three archangels who fought for God, in the beginning of creation, against the evil one. Lord, sometimes we need you to be by our side and fight for us. Send your angel during those difficult times.

All: Lord, send your angels to guide us.

Reader: Amen.

Thursday, First Week of Advent

Reader: Lord, send your angels to guide us.

All: Lord, send your angels to guide us.

Reader: Angel Gabriel, it was you who appeared to Saint Joseph, to the shepherds, and to Jesus in the garden. You bring God's message of hope. Lord God, fill our family with hope this Advent. We will place our hope in the coming of the baby Jesus.

All: Lord, send your angels to guide us.

Reader: Amen.

Friday, First Week of Advent

Reader: Lord, send your angels to guide us.

All: Lord, send your angels to guide us.

Reader: Angel Gabriel, in the gospels, you announce yourself and proclaim that you stand before God. Lord God, help us also to "stand before you." When we assemble the family crèche, we stand before you and pray: "Lord, surround us with your peace and glory."

All: Lord, send your angels to guide us.

Reader: Amen.

Saturday, First Week of Advent

Reader: Lord, send your angels to guide us.

All: Lord, send your angels to guide us.

Reader: Angel Gabriel, you are the most important of God's messengers because you carry the news of Jesus' birth. Lord God, help our family this Advent to be messengers of the news of Jesus' birth. We will show this news in our love for one another.

All: Lord, send your angels to guide us.

Reader: Amen.

WEEK TWO
Theme for Week Two

"Joseph, son of David, do not be afraid to take Mary as your wife, for the child conceived in her is from the Holy Spirit" (Mt 1:20).

Sunday, Second Week of Advent

Reader: Saint Joseph, watch over us.

All: Saint Joseph, watch over us.

Reader: Lord God, you chose Saint Joseph to be the human father of Jesus and the husband of Mary. Saint Joseph, look after our fathers and our grandfathers. Keep them safe and holy this Advent season.

All: Saint Joseph, watch over us.

Reader: Amen.

Monday, Second Week of Advent

Reader: Saint Joseph, watch over us.

All: Saint Joseph, watch over us.

Reader: Saint Joseph, you looked after and protected Mary and Jesus. Look after us, this Advent, as we prepare for the coming of Jesus. Be the extra eyes and the extra hands that see us and touch us.

All: Saint Joseph, watch over us.

Reader: Amen.

Tuesday, Second Week of Advent

Reader: Saint Joseph, watch over us.

All: Saint Joseph, watch over us.

Reader: Saint Joseph, God communicated with you in a dream and you listened. During this Advent, when our family goes to church, help us listen when God speaks to us. God will tell us that the Son is coming. Saint Joseph, open our ears to hear God's words.

All: Saint Joseph, watch over us.

Reader: Amen.

Wednesday, Second Week of Advent

Reader: Saint Joseph, watch over us.

All: Saint Joseph, watch over us.

Reader: Saint Joseph, you provided a house for Mary and Jesus in Nazareth. Be with us, Saint Joseph, as we prepare our home for Christmas. Let your presence be in our Christmas-tree decorating, our Advent-wreath celebrations, and our gift-giving. Fill our home with a spirit of holy warmth.

All: Saint Joseph, watch over us.

Reader: Amen.

Thursday, Second Week of Advent

Reader: Saint Joseph, watch over us.

All: Saint Joseph, watch over us.

Reader: Saint Joseph, you guided Mary from Nazareth to the town of Bethlehem. It was there that Jesus was born. Saint Joseph, guide our family through the pathways of Advent. Let us remain close to Mary and the child Jesus as we prepare for Christmas.

All: Saint Joseph, watch over us.

Reader: Amen.

Friday, Second Week of Advent

Reader: Saint Joseph, watch over us.

All: Saint Joseph, watch over us.

Reader: Saint Joseph, you were a carpenter. You spent your days building and your evenings talking to Mary and teaching the child Jesus. Help us, Saint Joseph, to use our gifts to build love, peace, and forgiveness in our family. Help us talk to and teach one another.

All: Saint Joseph, watch over us.

Reader: Amen.

Saturday, Second Week of Advent

Reader: Saint Joseph, watch over us.

All: Saint Joseph, watch over us.

Reader: Saint Joseph, when it looked like Herod was going to harm your family, you led them to safety. You trusted that God would know the way. Saint Joseph, be with our family when we are confused and do not know the way. Draw us together and lead us to safety.

All: Saint Joseph, watch over us.

Reader: Amen.

Week Three
Theme for Week Three

"Do not be afraid, Mary, for you have found favor with God"
(Lk: 1:30).

Sunday, Third Week of Advent

Reader: Mary, lead us to love.

All: Mary, lead us to love.

Reader: Mary, the angel of God came to you with a special message of love. You had to let go of your fear and love the new baby God gave you. Mary, help us love one another as God's special gifts. Help us look at our family members as God's special message of love.

All: Mary, lead us to love.

Reader: Amen.

Monday, Third Week of Advent

Reader: Mary, lead us to love.

All: Mary, lead us to love.

Reader: Mary, you are the mother of the baby Jesus, and our mother, too. Please bless all the women in our family, especially our mothers and grandmothers. Lead them to care for us with great love and closeness.

All: Mary, lead us to love.

Reader: Amen.

Tuesday, Third Week of Advent

Reader: Mary, lead us to love.

All: Mary, lead us to love.

Reader: Mary, when you heard God asking you to be the mother of Jesus, you said you would do whatever God wanted. Help us, during Advent, to listen and to do what God asks of us.

All: Mary, lead us to love.

Reader: Amen.

Wednesday, Third Week of Advent

Reader: Mary, lead us to love.

All: Mary, lead us to love.

Reader: Mary, it must have been very difficult for you to travel all the way to Bethlehem when Jesus was so close to being born. Mary, your love can help us do difficult things in our family. Help us, Mary, to think of you when we are asked to do difficult things.

All: Mary, lead us to love.

Reader: Amen.

Thursday, Third Week of Advent

Reader: Mary, lead us to love.

All: Mary, lead us to love.

Reader: Mary, you gave birth to Jesus in a stable. You were able to bless this little barn and make it holy. The stable became a special place. Mary, bless our home. Make it a special place. Help us, during Advent, do all we can to make our home a holy place.

All: Mary, lead us to love.

Reader: Amen.

Friday, Third Week of Advent

Reader: Mary, lead us to love.

All: Mary, lead us to love.

Reader: Mary, you wrapped Jesus in swaddling clothes after he was born to keep him warm. So many times, Mary, we might feel cold or forgotten. We need you to wrap us in your love. Help us, this Advent, wrap the other members of our family in love.

All: Mary, lead us to love.

Reader: Amen.

Saturday, Third Week of Advent

Reader: Mary, lead us to love.

All: Mary, lead us to love.

Reader: Mary, you raised Jesus and taught him how to love, how to live in a family, and how to care for others. Mary, continue to teach us, as you did Jesus. When we look at you with the baby Jesus, we will say: "Mary, love and teach us as you did Jesus."

All: Mary, lead us to love.

Reader: Amen.

WEEK FOUR
Theme for Week Four

"To you is born this day in the city of David a Savior, who is the Messiah, the Lord" (Lk 2:11).

Sunday, Fourth Week of Advent

Reader: Jesus, be our Light.

All: Jesus, be our Light.

Reader: Jesus, when you were born, a new star appeared in the sky. The star proclaimed that you are the Light of the World. Jesus, be the light of our family. Shine over us and let us see your great light.

All: Jesus, be our Light.

Reader: Amen.

Monday, Fourth Week of Advent

Reader: Jesus, be our Light.

All: Jesus, be our Light.

Reader: Jesus, you were born at night. Were you scared to come into a dark world? At times, our family is scared. Sometimes life seems dark for our family. When we feel this way, Lord, give us your courage.

All: Jesus, be our Light.

Reader: Amen.

Tuesday, Fourth Week of Advent

Reader: Jesus, be our Light.

All: Jesus, be our Light.

Reader: Jesus, as a little baby, you needed the care and protection of your parents. We also need the care and protection of our parents and caregivers. Touch them, Lord, so they may love us even more.

All: Jesus, be our Light.

Reader: Amen.

Wednesday, Fourth Week of Advent

Reader: Jesus, be our Light.

All: Jesus, be our Light.

Reader: Jesus, when you were born you were called Prince of Peace. You came to bring peace to our hearts, to our lives, and to our world. Jesus, bring your peace to our family this day.

All: Jesus, be our Light.

Reader: Amen.

Thursday, Fourth Week of Advent

Reader: Jesus, be our Light.

All: Jesus, be our Light.

Reader: Jesus, shepherds and kings rejoiced in your birth. They knew you were the God who came to save all people. You heal the lame and bring sight to the blind. Jesus, our family is very happy because you were born.

All: Jesus, be our Light.

Reader: Amen.

Friday, Fourth Week of Advent

Reader: Jesus, be our Light.

All: Jesus, be our Light.

Reader: Jesus, you laid in a manger, with straw to warm you. We lay in beds of cotton, but we also need to keep warm. Jesus, make our family a place of warmth. Help us wrap one another in a blanket of love.

All: Jesus, be our Light.

Reader: Amen.

Saturday, Fourth Week of Advent

Reader: Jesus, be our Light.

All: Jesus, be our Light.

Reader: Jesus, the kings came to worship you even though you were only a baby. We also worship you this Christmas. You are our baby King.

All: Jesus, be our Light.

Reader: Amen.

Christmas

All: "Glory to God in the highest heaven" (Lk 2:14).

Reader: Jesus, be our King.

All: Jesus, be our King.

Reader: Jesus, today, when you are born, the angels play their song of joy. Our family celebrates your birth, and we say with the angels: "Glory to God in the highest heaven."

All: Jesus, be our King.

Reader: Amen.

Advent Essays: The Church Waits

S ome of the great themes of Advent are suggested by the prophet Isaiah. In this season of preparation, as the Church waits for the coming of the Lord, it is helpful to recall Jesus' promise of peace, and helpful to renew our commitment to the poor and to ask for the necessary grace to triumph over fear as we reach for the Light that is Jesus. The short essays that follow offer some helpful points of reflection that may serve as a starting point for even more reflection and meditation.

1. The Prophecy and the Promise

"They shall beat their swords into plowshares, and their spears into pruning hooks" (Isa 2:4).

This vision presented by the prophet Isaiah is appealing. Who among us would not like to see all weapons of violence, no matter what form they may take, retooled into instruments of peace? Who would not like to see the day when the experience of violence is a distant memory?

In order for the vision of Isaiah to actually take root in our hearts and become part of our experience, a dramatic attitude shift is necessary. Such a shift demands that we realize violence is not waged only by a select few in isolated neighborhoods, or only in certain parts of the world. Violence flows out of a collective consciousness that accepts it, and the use of force, as a viable alternative. Violence would be significantly reduced, if not eliminated, if it were not tolerated, and, in some cases, not encouraged.

The vision presented by Isaiah is not likely, although it has been promised, because something within us clings to old ideas and solutions. Such ideas and solutions, tired and ineffective as they have demonstrated themselves to be, can only be replaced if new ideas are enthusiastically embraced as the old ideas once were. Recent examples have demonstrated this point. The way of nonviolence, for example, for a people faced with oppression, was exemplified in the lives of Mohandas Ghandi in India and Martin Luther King, Jr., in the United States.

The new ideas that must replace the old idea in this case is an individual commitment to listen, communicate, and discern; and finally, we must persevere in repeating this process again and again. In addition to such a commitment, a constant examination of our own choices, actions, and impulses, when faced with something we do not like would also be helpful. It is only in this way that the "old idea" can be replaced with a "new idea" of respectful tolerance, which can then lead to the experience of peace.

The season of Advent is when we celebrate the "already and the not yet" of who we are as a Christian people. This eschatological principle means that we have already received the promises of the Christ Child, simply because he came among us, but we have not yet experienced the fullness of each promise. We already know that which has been prophesied for us by Isaiah, but we have yet experienced the reality of that promise.

Would it be helpful to suggest, for our Advent reflection, that the Church waits for that which has been promised, and longs for that which is not yet here? We long for the day when swords and spears will be gone and the experience of peace will be ordinary. The church hopes. The church expects that this will one day be true.

2. Challenged by the Poor

"He shall judge the poor with justice, and decide aright for the land's afflicted" (Isa 11:4).

In every major city, the poor and the destitute are easily discovered, and not only in the neighborhoods or ghettos where we expect to find them. Increasingly, the poor and the destitute seem to be everywhere. It is not unusual to see a person begging on a street corner, sleeping in a doorway or in a park, or knocking on your door asking for a handout.

When unexpectedly confronted by such a person, different reactions occur in each of us. For some, it means walking a little faster so as not to be approached. Still others find themselves avoiding street corners, parks, or whole city blocks to avoid an unpleasant encounter.

Such reactions suggest a response based on the adage, "out of sight, out of mind," as a way of dealing with a difficult reality. Such a response, although tempting, is not the one suggested to us by the Gospel we profess to believe in. In the kingdom of God there is no such thing as "out of sight, out of mind." We are called to something more.

The ministry of Jesus, from its beginnings in Bethlehem, clearly focused on the poor and the destitute. The people who were oppressed, unwanted, and unloved were people in whom the Word took root, just as the Word took flesh among us. It was to just such a people that the promises of the kingdom were proclaimed. It was to just such a people that the kingdom made sense, and by whom it was welcomed and celebrated.

But again, the eschatological principle of "the already and the not yet" comes into play. Although it was to the poor that Jesus was sent, and to the poor that the kingdom was preached, the poor have not yet received the fullness of that which was preached and promised. In fact, the poor have received much less than what they had hoped for and imagined. The justice prophesied by Isaiah and promised by Jesus still seems so very far away.

The season of Advent calls each of us to a response in faith, particularly regarding concerns of justice and peace. It is easy to suggest such a call with the focus we experience in the readings from the prophet Isaiah and from the ever-present suggestion of the season we celebrate. This holiday season seems to call each of us to a special concern for the poor and the oppressed. Why else would there be the ringing of the bell and the Salvation Army kettles, the Tree of Lights, the Wreath of Hope, and all those other fund-raising efforts that daily surround us?

A possible Advent challenge might be to discover a way to make this seasonal concern and effort less occasional, and more of an individual, everyday effort. Might it not be a gospel truth to proclaim that it is for this very effort that the Church waits? Might it not be for this experience that the Church hopes? Might it not be that the Church expects that it one day to be true?

3. Triumph Over Our Fear

"Say to those who are frightened: be strong and fear not" (Isa 35:4).

The neighborhood in which I live in is a mixed ethnic neighborhood, a neighborhood that can be found in any large city, in any part of the world. Not only do such neighborhoods provide ethnic diversity but also a cultural, economic, and social blend. What we do not have in common is obvious; what we have in common is a little harder to discover.

One thing we do have in common, besides being neighbors, is a commitment to security devices. Our neighborhood is filled with house alarms, car alarms, movement-sensitive lights, and all the rest. In addition, we have a neighborhood watch program and keep a good working relationship with the district police. Yet all of our programs and all of our devices are not enough.

One evening, a neighbor, returning home from a parish council meeting just two short blocks away for her home, was gunned down in the street—on my well-lit, security-deviced street. There was no apparent reason for what happened: no leads that could be followed, no motive that made sense. All we know is that a neighbor was randomly shot and will be paralyzed for the rest of her life.

"Be strong and fear not," the prophet proclaims. But how can one not be fearful, I ask? Does not the evidence around me suggest that fear is a most appropriate response to what I see and feel? Fear certainly is prevalent in my neighborhood.

An easy answer to my pondering would be to suggest that the prophet was speaking of something more profound than my experience of fear. Yet another might be to suggest that the prophet was trying to make a theological point not immediately applicable to my present experience. But is that not exactly the point? Isn't my present lived experience exactly the place where faith needs to make sense? If I explain away the Word of God as something not being immediately applicable to my lived experience, when does the Word become applicable? At what point does what I believe have something to say about the way I live?

The season of Advent suggests to us that the point where faith and life become applicable can be found in the event for which we now prepare. "The Word became flesh, and dwelt among us" is the focal point. This God becoming flesh is supposed to inform not only our theology but also our everyday experience of life. There is supposed to be something for each of us in the mystery for which we prepare, something that is supposed to make a difference.

Again, we come to the eschatological truth of Advent. We have already received the promise of a life free of fear, but we have not yet experienced its fullness. Our Advent reflection leads us to a commitment, in our actions, in our choices, to empower the gospel truth for which the Church waits. We acknowledge that we live in hope for that day when fear will no longer be present; and we expect that hope to one day be fulfilled.

4. A Light in the Darkness

"The virgin shall be with child, and bear a son, and shall name him Emmanuel" (Isa 7:14).

A newborn baby; clean and fresh and peacefully resting in the arms of its mother. Even the most hardened among us cannot help but respond with a special joy when presented with such a picture. There is something about the miracle of life, made even more wonderful for us when we witness new life in a world where the violent termination of life is a distinct possibility. The new life in the arms of a mother speaks to us of innocence, of hope, and of almost unlimited potential.

Quickly tempering our initial feeling, however, is the stark reality of life. We are well aware that not all newborn life has a realistic chance for anything but the smallest joys this earthly pilgrimage offers us. Some children, born into abject poverty, will never recover from this accident of birth. Still others, possessed with a deadly disease, will spend most of their short lives fighting the ravages of their particular infirmity. It is only a small minority of newborns, mostly concentrated in what we casually refer to as the First World, who have any realistic hope of fulfilling all, or at least a good portion, of what we might dream or imagine for them.

The child prophesied by Isaiah was to be born in circumstances that were not at all promising. The child prophesied by Isaiah was to be born of poor and illiterate parents, in a country oppressed by an occupying army, into a race that was discriminated against and unjustly persecuted. Yet, despite this reality, Isaiah prophesied that in the birth of Emmanuel, the people would find hope. He prophesied that, despite the appearance of things, something else was possible, indeed probable, in the divine plan for God's people. Here is a message that has meaning for us today.

Our Advent reflection can lead us to discover the truth of what Isaiah prophesied. Our reflection can and should lead us to a firmer conviction of faith and belief in the dreams, the vision, and the hope of the promised child. It is in Jesus, the Emmanuel prophesied, that we can discover what it is we most wait for. It is in Jesus that we can expect to experience that which our hearts desire and for which our spirits cry out. It is in Jesus that the Church, each one of us, can expect to discover the way that leads to justice; the truth that leads to freedom; the life that is everlasting.

This Christmas, as we once again experience the new life promised in the birth of the Christ Child, we, too, can feel that nothing is impossible. In the birth of the Christ Child, prepared for during this season of Advent, we can rediscover and rekindle our own unique sense of innocence and hope, and the belief that all is possible with God.

The Church waits. The Church hopes. The Church expects that it will one day be true.

SECTION FIVE

Prayers Appropriate
for Advent

1. Act of Faith

O my God, I firmly believe that you are one God in three divine Persons, Father, Son, and Holy Spirit; I believe that your divine Son became man and died for our sins, and that he will come to judge the living and the dead. I believe these and all the truths, which the holy Catholic Church teaches, because you revealed them, who can neither deceive nor be deceived. Amen.

2. Act of Hope

O my God, relying on your infinite goodness and promises, I hope to obtain pardon of my sins, the help of your grace, and life everlasting, through the merits of Jesus Christ, my Lord and Redeemer. Amen.

3. Act of Love

O my God, I love you above all things, with my whole heart and soul, because you are all good and worthy of all my love. I love my neighbor as myself for the love of you. I forgive all that have injured me and I ask pardon of all whom I have injured. Amen.

4. Act of Contrition

My God, I am sorry for my sins with all my heart. In choosing to do wrong and failing to do good, I have sinned against you whom I should love above all things. I firmly intend, with your help, to do penance, to sin no more, and to avoid whatever leads me to sin. Our Savior Jesus Christ suffered and died for us. In his name, my God, have mercy. Amen.

5. Prayer for the Poor Souls in Purgatory

O Lord God almighty, I pray by the Precious Blood which the divine Jesus shed in his suffering, to deliver the souls in purgatory, and in particular that one which may be the last to depart, so that it may come before you to praise you in your glory and bless you for ever. Amen.

6. Confiteor (Traditional)

I confess to Almighty God, to blessed Mary ever Virgin, to blessed Michael the Archangel, to blessed John the Baptist, to the holy apostles Peter and Paul, to all the Saints, and to you Father, that I have sinned exceedingly in thought, word, and deed, through my fault, through my fault, through my most grievous fault (*here strike your breast three times*) therefore I beseech the blessed Mary ever Virgin, the blessed Michael the Archangel, the blessed John the Baptist, the holy apostles Peter and Paul, all the saints, and you Father, to pray to the Lord our God for me. May God have mercy on me, forgive me my sins, and lead me on to eternal life. Amen.

7. Prayer Before Confession

Lord Jesus, open my mind and my heart to your Holy Spirit. Show me where I am failing to love your heavenly Father. Show me where I am failing to love you, failing to accept you as my savior, failing to seek you and yield to you as my Lord. Show me where I am failing to love the Holy Spirit, failing to be open and to be led by Wisdom and Love.

Lord, Jesus, show me where I am failing to love any one of your brothers or sisters as you love me. Show me where I am failing to love myself as you love me. Show me where I am putting myself before God. Show me where I am seeking my own desires at the expense of a brother or a sister.

Your power finds its strength in my weakness; without you I can do nothing. Amen.

8. Prayer of Healing and Transformation

My love is like a wave breaking on the shore of eternity, forever washing over your weakness and wounds.
My mercy endures forever.

Every time you fail, I will forgive and heal you. Alone you can do nothing. With me you can do everything.

Let my grace transform you and heal your heart.

Know that I make everything work together for the good of those who love me. I can transform even your weaknesses and failures into blessings if you allow me.

Believe that you are filled with the healing presence of my Spirit.

Enter into my heart of divine compassion and let my love light a healing fire within your soul.

I release my power in your life now, and you will continue to grow in the depths and heights of my love.

Be at peace, my beloved, I am the God who dwells within you and embraces you with tenderness forever. Amen.

9. Traditional Examination of Conscience

The thorough examination of a person's conscience has been a traditional recommendation for those who are preparing for the confession of their sins. Within the spiritual tradition of the Church, there are occasions when the examination should be very detailed in preparation for the celebration of the sacrament. One such occasion when a detailed examination should take place is within the season of Advent.

The detailed examination of conscience begins with a prayer and a series of preparatory questions and then examines the person in relation to the Ten Commandments and the Precepts of the Church. The detailed examination ends with particular questions for people in different "states in life," such as married, single, or religious and, finally, particular questions for people who are doctors, lawyers, pharmacists, and so on. The examination that follows is from *The Mission Book of the Redemptorist Fathers,* a devotional manual routinely used by many Catholics until the Second Vatican Council. The examination will include edited questions pertaining to the Ten Commandments and the Precepts of the Church but will not include the questions for people in different states in life.

PREPARATORY PRAYER

O God, Father of light, who enlightens everyone that comes into this world, give me light, love and sorrow, that I may discover, detest and confess all the sins that I have committed.

O Most holy Virgin Mary, Mother of the Redeemer, so compassionate towards those who desire to repent, help me to make a good confession.

My dear Guardian Angel, help me to call to mind all my offenses. All the saints and angels, pray for me that I may now bring forth worthy fruits of penance.

PREPARATORY QUESTIONS

How long ago did you make your last confession? Did you receive absolution? Have you performed your penance? Did you willfully conceal a mortal sin or confess without true sorrow, without the purpose of amendment, or without intending to perform your penance?

First Commandment: I am the Lord your God, you shall have no gods before me.

Have you disbelieved or willfully indulged in doubts against any article of faith or suggested or encouraged such doubts in others? Have you attended or joined in false worship? Have you exposed your faith to danger by evil associations? Have you remained a long time, a whole month or longer, without reciting any prayer, or performing any act of devotion towards God? Have you consulted fortunetellers or made use of superstitious practices, love potions, or charms?

Second Commandment: You shall not take the name of the Lord your God in vain.

Have you been guilty of blasphemy by angry, injurious, or insulting words against God? Have you pronounced in a blasphemous or irreverent manner, or in anger, the holy name of God, the name of Jesus Christ, or that of any of the saints? Have you sworn a false oath? Have you cursed yourself or cursed a neighbor?

Third Commandment: Remember to keep holy the Sabbath day.
How often have you on Sundays and holy days of obligation willfully choose not to attend Mass, or come too late, or leave before Mass was over? How often have you performed unnecessary servile work on Sundays and on holy days or caused others to do the same? How often did you desecrate these days by frequenting ungodly company, by sinful amusements, gambling, immodest dancing, or drinking to excess?

Fourth Commandment: Honor your father and your mother.

Have you insulted, mocked, ridiculed, or cursed your parents? Have you threatened them, or even lifted your hand to strike them? Have you sorely grieved your parents by your ingratitude or misconduct? Have you neglected or refused to aid them in their wants? Have you neglected to pray for them? Have you neglected to pray for the repose of their souls?

Fifth Commandment: You shall not kill.

Have you by act, participation, instigation, counsel, or consent been guilty of anyone's death or bodily injury? Have you intended or attempted to take another's life? Have you injured your health by excess in eating or drinking? Have you been drunk or been the cause of drunkenness in another? Have you by act, advice, or consent done anything to hinder or destroy life? Have you harmed the soul of another person by giving scandal? Have you by wicked words, deeds or bad example, ruined innocent persons, taught them bad habits or things they should not know?

Sixth and Ninth Commandments: You shall not commit adultery and you shall not covet your neighbors' wife.

These commandments forbid everything that is contrary to purity. How often have you made use of impure language, allusions, or words of double meaning? How often have you voluntarily exposed yourself to the occasion of sin by sinful curiosity, by frequenting dangerous company, places, or sinful amusements? How often have you been guilty of improper liberties with others? Have far have you carried your sinful conduct? You must mention those circumstances that change the nature of your sin—the sex, the relationship, and the condition—whether married, single, or bound by vow. Were you married or single at the time?

Seventh and Tenth Commandments: You shall not steal and you shall not covet your neighbors' goods.

Have you stolen money or anything of value? Is it still in your possession? What was its value? How much did you take each time and how often? Have you stolen anything belonging to God or to a sacred place? Have you charged exorbitant prices, or made out false bills, or cheated in the weight, measure, quantity, or quality of your goods? Have you cheated in games? Have you been guilty of forgery? Have you kept things you found without inquiring for the owner? Have you bought, received, or concealed things you knew to be stolen?

Eighth Commandment: You shall not bear false witness against your neighbor.

Have you taken a false oath or advised others to do so? Have you signed false papers or forged writings? Have you been guilty of malicious lying? Have you caused ill feelings between others by tale-bearing? Have you attempted to repair the harm you have done by contradicting your false reports? Have you been guilty of unjust suspicions and rash judgments?

10. Visit to the Most Blessed Sacrament: Saint Alphonsus Liguori

At one time, in the not-so-distant past, the practice of a daily visit to the Blessed Sacrament was not uncommon. The faithful on their way home from the fields would stop in the village church or coming home from work they would stop in the neighborhood church. Priests, monks, and religious women, living in monasteries and convents with chapels, would often stop into the chapel in the midst of their daily routine and make a quick visit to the Blessed Sacrament. Unfortunately this practice, because of a variety of reasons, fell into disfavor. Today, however, the practice is being revived with a renewed interest, because of the establishment of the practice of Perpetual Adoration in many parish churches and because of a renewed emphasis on the doctrine of the True Presence of Christ in the Blessed Sacrament.

The *Visits to the Blessed Sacrament* by Saint Alphonsus is a perennial favorite. Each visit (the saint provides the faithful with an appropriate visit for each day of the month) consists of an opening prayer, a meditation on the Eucharist, a spiritual communion prayer, a visit to the Blessed Mother, and finally a closing prayer.

OPENING PRAYER

My Lord Jesus Christ, I believe that you are really here in this sacrament. Night and day you remain here compassionate and loving. You call, you wait for, and you welcome, everyone who comes to you.

Unimportant though I am, I adore you. I thank you for all the wonderful graces you have given me. But I thank you especially for having given me yourself in this sacrament, for having asked your own Mother to mother me, for having called me here to talk to you.

I am here before you today to do three things: to thank you for these precious gifts, to make up for all the disrespect that you receive in this sacrament from those who offend you, to adore you everywhere in the world where you are present in this living bread but are left abandoned and unloved.

My Jesus, I love you with all my heart. I know I have displeased you often in the past—I am sorry. With your help I promise never to do it again. I am only a miserable sinner, but I consecrate myself to you completely. I give you my will, my love, my desires, everything I own. From now on do what you please with me. All I ask is that you love me, that you keep me faithful to the end of my life. I ask for the grace to do your will exactly as you want it done.

I pray for the souls in purgatory—especially for those who were close to you in this sacrament and close to your mother Mary. I pray for every soul hardened in sin. My Savior, I unite my love to the love of your divine heart, and I offer them both together to your Father. I beg him to accept this offering in your name. Amen.

VISIT APPROPRIATE FOR ADVENT

The spouse in the Song of Songs searches for her lover with these words: Have you see him whom my soul loves? Christ had not as yet come to live in the world. If his lovers are lonely for him now, they need only turn to the Bread of Life on the altar. A holy priest claimed that he found no place more peaceful or more restful than before a tabernacle that houses Christ.

O boundless Lover, you deserve to be boundlessly loved! To keep us company and unite yourself to our hearts, you have hidden divine dignity under the form of bread! How could you ever humble yourself so deeply? Your humility is fathomless because it matches the depths of your love.

I marvel at all the measures you have taken to captivate my love. I cannot refuse to love you. I promise that your love shall come before self-interest, self-satisfaction, and self-gratification. I will find pleasure in pleasing you, my God. Make me hunger and crave to feed on the Eucharist and to continually keep you company. Only the coldest of hearts could reject the warmth of your love.

Crush every affection in me that clings to worldly things, Lord. You want my love, my desires, and my affections, directed toward yourself alone. I love you, and I beg nothing for myself. My pleasure is to please you. Accept this desire of a stumbling sinner who really wants to love you. Help me with your powerful graces. Change me from a sinner to a saint. Amen.

SPIRITUAL COMMUNION

My Jesus, I believe you are really here in the Blessed Sacrament. I love you more than anything in the world, and I hunger to feed on your flesh. But since I cannot receive communion at this moment, feed my soul at least spiritually. I unite myself to you now as I do when I actually receive you. Never let me be parted from you.

VISIT WITH MARY

My gentle Mother, I have disgracefully rebelled against your Son. I am sorry for what I have done. I kneel at your feet, hoping that you will obtain pardon for me. I know you can do so because Saint Bernard calls you the "minister of forgiveness." But I am confident that you will supply me with everything I need: courage to ask forgiveness, perseverance, and heaven. I hope to praise your mercy forever, my Queen, for having gained heaven through your ministry.

CONCLUDING PRAYER

Most Holy Immaculate Virgin and my Mother Mary, to you who are the Mother of my Lord, the Queen of the world, the Advocate, the Hope, the Refuge of Sinners, I have recourse today—I who am the most miserable of all. I render you my most humble homage, O great Queen, and I thank you for all the graces you have conferred on me until now, particularly for having delivered me from hell, which I have so often deserved. I love you, O most amiable Lady; and for the love that I bear you, I promise to serve you always and to do all in my power to make others also love you. I place in you all my hopes; I confide my salvation to your care. Accept me for your servant and receive me under your mantle, O Mother of Mercy. And since you are so powerful with God, deliver me from all temptations, or rather obtain for me the strength to triumph over them until death. Of you I ask a perfect love for Jesus Christ. From you I hope to die a good death. O my Mother, by the love which you bear to God, I beseech you to help me at all times, but especially at the last moment of my life. Leave me not, I beseech you, until you see me safe in heaven, blessing you and singing your mercies for all eternity. Amen. So I hope. So may it be.

11. Light for All the World

Almighty God, Creator of heaven and earth, we believe that you are our Father, and that you can make us your children, who are worthy of you as brothers and sisters who lead one another closer to you and walk in your light.

We believe that you have shared all your wisdom, your holiness, and your love with your Son, your eternal Word. By sending him to be our brother, you have given us everything.

We believe in Jesus Christ, Light of Light, true God, and true human. Through him and in him, we share in your own life.

We believe that you have called us into your light by sending us your Son and the Spirit of Truth. If we entrust ourselves to you, and are guided by the Holy Spirit, we shall not walk in darkness. We will become, for each other, a humble light that points to you, the One who is Light of Light.

Father, we praise you for having glorified your Servant, Jesus Christ, who has given his life for his sisters and brothers. For all of us, you made him the source of everlasting life. We thank you for having called us to abide in Christ, and to be the salt of the earth and the light of the world. Amen.

SECTION SIX

Daily Meditations for Advent

A useful Advent spiritual practice that has proven to be quite popular is the commitment to a daily period of prayer and reflection. Although daily prayer and reflection is appropriate throughout the year, it seems to be especially appropriate during this spiritual season.

In the pages that follow, a collection of daily meditations for Advent, along with the assigned Scripture references for each day of the season, is arranged for personal use. You will notice that for the Sundays of Advent the Scripture citations for the entire liturgical cycle are listed for your convenience; the cycle on which the meditation is based is in bold italic print. The weekday meditations are provided for each day of the season. The O Antiphons, although they are proper as the antiphon for the recitation of the *Magnificat* (the Liturgy of the Hours, Evening Prayer) beginning on December 17, are nonetheless provided as a possible alternative meditation opportunity.

There are many different ways to use the meditations that are provided. A suggested format would include the following steps, often considered essential for fruitful prayer and meditation.

The first step is to choose a particular time each day for your prayer. It is also helpful to choose a particular place that is conducive to reflection and to assume a position that is comfortable. Many people find fifteen or twenty minutes first thing in the morning, before the household awakens, to be very beneficial.

The second step is to quietly read the assigned Scripture for the day. It is not necessary to read the entire Scripture reference, the point is not to get through everything, but rather to be open to the gentle proddings of the Spirit of God. Some people choose to read just the suggested gospel, others choose just a few lines of text and find it very satisfactory.

The third step is to take some quiet reflection time, just a few moments, and let the Word of God be present to you. After a few moments of quiet, you may then choose to read the meditation that is provided for the day. Again, after reading the meditation, take a few more moments of quiet.

The fourth step is to present to God, through prayers of petition, or thanks and praise, the fruits of your reflection. For example, the Scripture and the daily meditation might have helped you become aware of your gratefulness for the gift of life or the gift of family. A few simple words of praise and thanksgiving would then be appropriate. Or perhaps you became aware of a relationship that needs mending; a prayer for the other person in the relationship might be appropriate. Whatever comes to you in prayer is considered the voice of God or the "gentle prodding of the Holy Spirit."

The fifth step is to conclude your period of prayer and meditation with the slow recitation of a familiar prayer. Some people routinely choose to pray the Our Father. Still others might choose a prayer from the collections provided in Section Five of this handbook, "Prayers Appropriate for Advent."

1. Contemporary Meditations

First Sunday of Advent
Isa 2:1–5; Ps 122:1–9; Rom 13:11–14a; Mt 24:37–44 (Cycle A)

*Isa 63:16b–17, 19b; 64:2–7; Ps 80:2–3, 15–16, 18–19;
1 Cor 1:3–9; Mk 13:33–37 (Cycle B)*

*Jer 33:14–16; Ps 25:4–5, 8–9, 10, 14; 1 Thess 3:12–4:2;
Lk 21:25–28, 34–36 (Cycle C)*

> To you, O LORD, I lift up my soul.
> O my God, in you I trust.
> (Ps 25:1–2)

I was visiting a family during the Advent season whose young daughter was only eight weeks old. The parents with excitement placed the baby down in front of the Christmas tree and then turned on the Christmas-tree lights. The bulbs, tinsel, and lights of the tree exploded into the darkened room. The baby's face burst into smiles and giggles. Her eyes were focused on this new vision of twinkling stars. All the while that I spoke with the parents, the child lay transfixed.

In our readings for this First Sunday of Advent, the Scriptures invite us to become focused on the new light of Jesus that is coming into the world. The gospel tells us to beware that our hearts don't lose this vision through worry, distraction, or too much celebration. We are to be vigilant people, constantly fixed on God's signs of new life. Saint Paul tells us that if we remain focused then the Lord will increase our love for one another. As we place those shiny bulbs and tiny lights on the Christmas tree, let us pray: "Lord, give me eyes that see your sparkling beauty in every heart I meet today. Amen."

Monday of the First Week
Isa 2:1–5; Ps 122:1–9; Mt 8:5–11

For the sake of my relatives and friends
I will say, "Peace be within you."
(Ps 122:8)

In the first reading, Isaiah challenges us to walk in the paths of the Lord, to walk in the light of the Lord. What does this mean for us? Jesus in the gospel reminds us that to walk in the Lord's light is to be a person who waits upon the Lord's word, even if we are in need of great healing. We believe and wait. Isaiah is more direct and tells us that to walk in the Lord's light means that you are actively creating peace. Today we pray: "Lord, I await your healing word to me. Lead me to be a person of peace. Amen."

105

Tuesday of the First Week
Isa 11:1–10; Ps 72:1, 7–8, 12–13, 17; Lk 10:21–24

> *In his days may righteousness flourish*
> *and peace abound,*
> *until the moon is no more.*
> *(Ps 72:7)*

The Advent season is certainly a time for children. We buy presents for them, put the crib set up with them, and permit them to help us trim the tree, bake the cookies, and make the Advent wreath. In training and loving our children, we reach out and touch the future. Today's readings tell us of the hope we place in the child. Isaiah speaks to us of the child that will bring peace and justice to all life. In Luke's Gospel, Jesus tells us that we are to become like this child—a person who brings peace and justice. Let us pray today: "Lord, give me eyes of wonder that see your treasure of peace that is within my heart. Amen."

Wednesday of the First Week
Isa 25:6–10a; Ps 23:1–6; Mt 15:29–37

> *Surely goodness and mercy shall follow me*
> *all the days of my life.*
> *(Ps 23:6)*

If there ever is a time to believe in miracles, Advent season is that time! We hear of the miracle of Mary's conception, the miracle of Jesus' birth in a barn, the miracle of the star in the night sky leading the wise men. A saint whose feast is celebrated during the Advent season, Saint Nicholas, was often called the "wonder-worker." Even the Scriptures speak to us of God's miraculous and unceasing care for us. God always provides for us. Today let us believe in miracles and wonders. We Pray: "Lord, you are the God of wonders, bring a miracle into my life on this day! Amen."

Thursday of the First Week
Isa 26:1–6; Ps 118:1, 8–9, 19–21, 25–27; Mt 7:21, 24–27

> *Open to me the gates of righteousness,*
> *that I may enter through them.*
> *(Ps 118:19)*

A friend, returning from a desert retreat, told me that she had made a decision to do God's will. She was waiting for God to reveal a new direction for her life. The readings today present God offering us a gate, a passageway, into God's will. For Isaiah, the gateway to God consists in being just and keeping the faith. For Jesus, it is the person who hears God's word and puts those words into practice. When we listen to the Scriptures, let us pray: "Lord, open the gate of my heart. Let your words be a light that will lead me to follow your will. Amen."

Friday of the First Week
Isa 29:17–24, Ps 27:1, 4, 13–14, Mt 9:27–31

> *The LORD is my light and my salvation;*
> *whom should I fear.*
> *(Ps 27:1)*

We can easily identify with today's reading from Isaiah, because we *know* that when we awake our dreams are lost. The hungry who are filled in dreams wake up still hungry. Perhaps they remember their dream, but cannot remember their feeling of fullness. But we remember other dreams from Scripture, and realize that the wise *can* fulfill their dreams. Joseph's dreams led him to marriage and to Egypt. The blind men in today's gospel surely dreamed of being sighted, and those dreams were fulfilled through their perfect faith in Christ the Healer. Thus we do sing with the psalmist: "One thing I asked of the Lord, that I will seek after…[and]…I believe that I shall see the goodness of the Lord in the land of the living. Amen."

Saturday of the First Week
Isa 30:19–21, 23–26; Ps 147:1–6; Mt 9:35—10:1, 6–8

> *He heals the brokenhearted,*
> *and binds up their wounds.*
> *(Ps 147:3)*

Can you remember your favorite teacher in school? This teacher could inspire you, relate to you, encourage you, and challenge you. The book of Isaiah reveals God as such a teacher. God, our teacher, was once hidden but is now known. God is a teacher who will care for our every need, from filling our hunger to directing us in right paths. His disciples also call Jesus "teacher." Jesus chose them and taught them how to announce the reign of God. Jesus remains as our teacher. Jesus chooses us, directs us, and asks us to announce the good news on this day. Let us pray: "Lord, be my teacher on this day. Direct my words and actions. Amen!"

Second Sunday of Advent
Isa 11:1–10; Ps 72:1–2, 7–8, 12–13, 17; Rom 15:4–9,
Mt 3:1–12 (Cycle A)

Isa 40:1–5, 9–11; Ps 85:9–14; 2 Pet 3:8–14, Mk 1:1–8 (Cycle B)

Bar 5:1–9; Ps 126:1–2, 2–3, 4–6, 6; Phil 1:4–6, 8–11;
Lk 3:1–6 (Cycle C)

> *The LORD has done great things for us,*
> *and we rejoiced.*
> *(Ps 126:3)*

Every year during the advent season there is a television advertisement showing a handsome younger man and woman kneeling before the Christmas tree. All the lights of the tree are on and the tree is shown faded softly in the background. In the advertisement, the man gives the woman a beautifully packaged small box. She opens it. Inside is a magnificent diamond ring that out-sparkles the Christmas tree. In this ad, there is no speaking. But we know the message: "All the power of love is contained in this diamond ring" and "how right and beautiful it would be to give a diamond ring to someone you love."

In today's Scripture, the prophet Baruch speaks of God giving the chosen people a beautifully wrapped gift. What is this gift? Baruch tells us that the gift will bring light, mercy, justice, and glory. The gospel shows us that part of the gift is a diamond in the rough. It is John the Baptist coming out of the desert breathing the fire of repentance and dressed like an animal. This hints to us that the rest of the gift (Jesus at Christmas) will not be the perfect, shining diamond but will represent the rougher side of life. The poor, the lame, the outcast, and the sick will be part of the experience of the child Jesus in the stable and the adult Jesus on the hillside. We are asked to wear this rough diamond ring again this Christmas. To keep clear in our minds and hearts that we are to repent and await Jesus' liberation with all our poor sisters and brothers. We pray: "Lord, make straight the winding ways within me. Draw me to repent and believe in you more deeply on this day! Amen."

Monday of the Second Week
Isa 35:1–10; Ps 85:9–14; Lk 5:17–26

Faithfulness will spring up from the ground,
and righteousness will look down from the sky.
(Ps 85:11)

People who have entered a personal time of dryness and barrenness in their prayer life often describe this period as a "desert experience." Yet if you visit a desert, you will see that it is alive with plants, flowers, animals, and various soft scents. It is not a dead place at all. In today's Scripture, we are told that the desert within us will come alive. It will not be a barren place. In the gospel, Jesus proves this by giving life to the dead limbs of a paralytic. In Jesus all the prophecies of life springing from the barren desert find their fulfillment. We pray: "Lord to you we lift up our barrenness. Make it bloom with your love and life! Amen."

Tuesday of the Second Week
Isa 40:1–11; Ps 96:1–3, 10–13; Mt 18:12–14

The LORD God comes with might.
(Isa 40:10)

There have been a series of television programs recently showing dangerous and daring rescues. Helicopters pluck passengers from sinking ships and fireman carry babies from the burning buildings. These programs give the hope that if one ever needed to be rescued, no matter how dire the circumstances, someone would be there. Our Scriptures today overflow with this same hope. In the gospel, Jesus proclaims that he personally will rescue us. Even if we are the only one lost, he will come after us. The book of Isaiah tells us that our God is a God of comfort, carrying us in God's bosom. Are we in trouble? Are we lost? Are we confused or overwhelmed? Allow the Lord today to rescue you. Allow God to comfort you. Let us pray: "Lord, speak tenderly to me and proclaim to me that you will find me, gather me up in your arms, and rescue me. Amen!"

Wednesday of the Second Week
Isa 40:25–31; Ps 103:1–4, 8, 10; Mt 11:28–30

Bless the LORD, O my soul.
(Ps 103:1)

There are so very few constant things in our lives. Our bodies grow old, our children grow up, our homes and cars deteriorate, even our paper money fades. Is there a place to go for constancy and abiding strength? Our Scriptures present us with the anchor that never rusts, the eagle that always carries us, the lamb that lifts our burdens. It is the Lord! In the midst of the Advent rush, let us rely on the Lord to renew our strength, to carry our burdens, to always be a never- failing source of life for us. We pray: "O Lord we come to you. We are burdened and struggling. Make our vigor abound and lift us up on your wings. Amen!"

Thursday of the Second Week
Isa 41:13–20; Ps 145:1, 9–13; Mt 11:11–15

The LORD is good to all,
and his compassion is over all that he has made.
(Ps 145:9)

Every Advent, the toy industry presents their newest, most cutting-edge product. This latest toy is built to wow the children and to empty the parents' pocketbook. In the Old and New Testaments, God called various men and women to be "cutting-edge" ambassadors of God's word. It was their job to "wow" the people so that they would empty their pagan pocketbooks and return to the Lord. John the Baptist was such a prophet. He was a threshing sledge, a double-edged sword. He came to refocus us for the coming of the Lord. We pray: "Lord, empty me today of the many pre-Christmas expectations that distract my spirit. Help me refocus on God, my Savior, so that I may truly blossom. Amen!"

Friday of the Second Week
Isa 48:17–19; Ps 1:1–4, 6; Mt 11:16–19

Whoever follows me will never walk in darkness
but will have the light of life.
(Jn 8:12)

This is certainly a season of love. We wonder what gifts we will give to those we love. We wait in anticipation for the gifts we might receive from those who love us. People give more freely to charities because there is a feeling of love in the air. In our first reading today, Isaiah prophecies that if we listen to and obey God's commandments then prosperity will be ours. Jesus in the gospel calls the people to listen to his wisdom. Jesus' wisdom is the wisdom of love. Jesus' law is the law of love. It is his last command to his followers. We pray: "Lord, fill me with your love in this season. Today, I especially extend your love to my family, my friends, and my community. Amen!"

Saturday of the Second Week
Sir 48:1–4, 9–11; Ps 80:2–3, 15–16, 18–19; Mt 17:10–13

Restore us, O God;
let your face shine, that we may be saved.
(Ps 80:3)

A young lady told me that during the days of Advent she looks for the signs of Jesus' coming. Sometimes the cloud formations speak to her of the Holy Spirit or the flame of the Advent wreath candle becomes the twinkle in the eye of the baby Jesus. Today's Scriptures encourage us to look for the signs of Jesus, the new Elijah, who will restore life to us. So this Advent we wait, we watch, and we pray: "Lord, help me see the signs of your coming. Let me not be blinded by the glare of business or the millions of lights on the homes and trees. I will look for you in the small things of the day. Amen!"

Third Sunday of Advent
Isa 35:1–6, 10; Ps 146:6–10, Jas 5:7–10; Mt 11:2–11 (Cycle A)

Isa 61:1–2, 10–11; Lk 1:46–50, 53–54; 1 Thess 5:16–24; Jn 1:6–8, 19–28 (Cycle B)

Zep 3:14–18; Isa 12:2–6; Phil 4:4–7; Lk 3:10–18 (Cycle C)

As I live, says the LORD, every knee shall bow to me,
and every tongue shall give praise to God.
(Rom 14:11)

The Third Sunday of Advent signals a change. Called *Gaudete*, a Latin word meaning "rejoice," even the tenor of the readings sounds different. They are filled with promise; they bring hope to a people heavy under the burden of waiting. The liturgical trappings look different, too. A rose-colored candle is lit in the Advent wreath, and rose-colored vestments are worn for the liturgical celebration. The coming of the Lord draws closer.

"Here is your God," said Isaiah. "He will come and save you. Then the eyes of the blind shall be opened, and the ears of the deaf unstopped; then the lame shall leap like a deer, and the tongue of the speechless sing for joy." We hear Isaiah's prophecy fulfilled in Jesus' words today, as he answers John's inquiry made from prison, "Go and tell John what you hear and see."

James offered the same promise to his people as Isaiah had offered so long before, and yet Jesus had already died and risen before James wrote, so it is clear he did not expect the same "coming of the Lord" as Isaiah had. These folks were suffering for their faith in Jesus; the hope that James offered was for the Lord's Second Coming, which was not only hoped for but also imminently expected. Our hope today is also imminently filled with expectation; Jesus will come again, very soon.

Monday of the Third Week
Num 24:2–7, 15–17a; Ps 25:4–9; Mt 21:23–27

Make me to know your ways, O LORD;
teach me your paths.
(Ps 25:4)

If someone told you that they conversed with God and that they would reveal to you what God was saying, you might look at them as if they were crazy. Our present culture places little value on those who commune with the divine. Both readings today suggest that the Christian is one who listens to God. The prophet Balaam makes the claim that the future Jesus will hear what God says and know what God knows. Jesus, in the gospel, proves that this claim is right. Jesus is the one with divine authority. In the baby Jesus, the doors of the heavenly library are open to us. In and through Jesus, God will now speak to us. We pray: "Lord, speak to me this day, teach me your ways, let me see what God sees. Amen!"

Tuesday of the Third Week
Zep 3:1–2, 9–13; Ps 34:1–3, 5–6, 16–18, 22; Mt 21:28–32

The LORD is near to the brokenhearted,
and saves the crushed in spirit.
(Ps 34:18)

Are you in the core group of Christians who embody and live the purest form of the gospel? Or do you find yourself among the masses that acknowledge Jesus, enjoy being Christian, but don't pursue it at any deep level? Our readings today invite us to join the core Christians. How do you become a core member? The two requirements in the gospel are that you repent and you believe. If you do this, then you become part of the core remnant in today's reading from Zephaniah. These are the people that possess no deceit, do no wrong, and speak no lies. Let his Advent be a time when you begin the journey to the Christian core. We pray: "Lord, lead me to repent this day of my old ways, and to believe more deeply in you Amen!"

Wednesday of the Third Week
Isa 45, 6b–8, 18, 21b–25; Ps 85:9–14; Lk 7:18–23

Let me hear what God the LORD will speak,
for he will speak peace to his people.
(Ps 85:8)

Many times people talk about who is the most important person they have ever seen or met. The conversation usually points to politicians, popes, presidents, or movie stars. Both readings today ask us to focus this question on God and Jesus. We have met God! God is the Lord, and there is no other. Jesus tells John's disciples that he is the one that all of Israel has been waiting for. In this Advent season, we proclaim that we are waiting for and wanting Jesus to come into our world, our community, our family, and our heart. Jesus is the most important person in our lives. We need the creator of all life to re-create us again. We want the power of the entire universe that is born in a baby, to be born again within our fledgling spirits. We pray: "Lord, today I embrace you as my creator, my leader, and my savior. Dwell deeply within me now. Amen!"

Thursday of the Third Week
Isa 54:1–10; Ps 30:2–6, 10–12, 13; Lk 7:24–30

You have turned my mourning into dancing;
O LORD my God, I will give thanks to you forever.
(Ps 30:11, 12)

Many people long for change in their lives. Those in loveless marriages long for affection. Those with poor wages dream of better pay and higher position. Politicians scheme to be presidents, and teenagers yearn to be adults. Both readings today speak of change. Isaiah promises his people that the Messiah will change everything. All life will be better when the Savior arrives. In the gospel, Jesus speaks of the great change that happens in the kingdom of God. John the Baptist, dressed in animal fur and living in the desert, is the great messenger. The Pharisees, dressed in fine robes and living in palaces, are rejected. Advent is the time to ask Jesus to change us. Let the message of John the Baptist prepare us for the change that Jesus will bring. We pray: "Lord, come into my life this day. Change me. Restore me to your kingdom. Amen!"

Friday of the Third Week
Isa 56:1–3, 6–8; Ps 67:2–3, 5, 7–8; Jn 5:33–36

May God be gracious to us and bless us
and make his face to shine upon us.
(Ps 67:1)

Fortunetellers, soothsayers, and tarot-card readers prey upon our desire to know the future. Stock markets rise and fall on what people guess the future will bring. The Scripture today also gives us a way to unravel the future. Isaiah tells us that if we observe what is right and do what is just then a future of salvation, justice, and love will be revealed to us. Jesus invites us to testify, like John the Baptist, to the truth and then great works of Jesus will be unveiled for us to see. This Advent, we testify to Jesus who is the Light. Let us not be trapped by the commercialism, competitiveness, or depression that drives the materialism of this season. We challenge ourselves to be loving, kind, and giving of our goodness. Then the future will be ours to see. We pray: "Lord, today I hold you as my truth. You are my Light and my Hope. Lead me this day. Amen!"

Please Note

The weekday readings for the Advent season become date specific on December 17 each year. The earliest occurrence for this change is Monday of the Third Week of Advent. The meditations follow for the weekdays of Advent. For those years in which there is celebrated a Fourth Sunday of Advent, the meditation for the Fourth Sunday of Advent may be found in an appendix that follows the weekday meditations for December 17 to December 24.

December 17
Gen 49:2, 8–10; Ps 72:3–4, 7–8, 17; Mt 1:1–17

O come, Thou Wisdom from on High.
(Latin hymn, ninth century)

On a frosty and pitch-dark winter evening, I was returning from a Christmas shopping trip. At the stoplight was a man who held a cardboard sign stating: "Please, Anything will do!" These street people look especially vulnerable and weak during this Advent time. For so many people Advent is a time of depression and loneliness. They are strapped for money, out of work, without a home or family. This whole season sings of celebration yet many have nowhere to celebrate and no one to celebrate with. Our Scripture challenges us to reach inside of ourselves and find a deeper reason for joy and celebration. This reason must be richer and more moving than friends, family, or even homes. This reason must compel us to reach out to those in depression and loneliness to share our joy. The reason is proclaimed over and over in today's Scripture. It is that God's presence is in your midst, that God is near, that there is one who is to come and he is here. All the readings call to us to shout for joy, rejoice, and be full of anticipation because God is dawning on our world.

Joy is contagious! Your Advent rejoicing might be the switch that turns another from darkness to light. So today rejoice fully in the Lord's presence. We pray: "Lord, I am awash in your presence. You are light. You are goodness. Fill me and my world with your life this day. Amen!"

December 18
Jer 23:5–8; Ps 72:1–2, 7a, 12–13, 18–19; Mt 1:18–24

O come, O come, great Lord of might.
(Latin hymn, ninth century)

Today the Lord of might comes into our life. Our Scripture reminds us of the various ways that the Lord of might acts in our favor. It is the Lord who is our justice. It is the Lord who leads us away from places of slavery into places of freedom. It is the Lord who brings holy life into a virgin's womb and will bring life to our barrenness. It is the Lord who speaks to Joseph in dreams and who will speak to us. It is the Lord who names Jesus: Emmanuel (God with us). We pray: "Lord, free me from any slavery, fill me with new life, speak to me in my sleeping and my waking. Amen!"

December 19
Jgs 13:2–7, 24–25a; Ps 71:3–4a, 5–6, 8, 16–17; Lk 1:5–25

O come, O come, O Flower of Jesse stem.
(Latin hymn, ninth century)

In many ancient Christian hymns, Jesus is portrayed as a flower that is fully blossoming. Jesus is the great flower that comes from the stem of Jesse (from the Israelite people). In today's Scripture we witness the power of God which keeps fertility alive. We are shown the miraculous births of Samson and John the Baptist. How many times in our lives have we felt barren and lifeless? We need God to give us a miraculous new birthing. We pray for that birthing this day: "Lord, touch my barrenness and make me into a blossoming flower once again. Amen!"

December 20
Isa 7:10–14; Ps 24:1–6, 7b, 10b; Lk 1:26–38

O come, O Key of David, come!
(Latin hymn, ninth century)

How many times have you reached the door of your home and found yourself fumbling for the right key? This task is all the more frustrating when we are hauling food bags and presents. It is such a relief when we finally swing that door open and lay down our load. God speaks to the house of David today and tells them that God will send a key that will open the door that separates God from his people. This key is Jesus. In the gospel, God fulfills this ancient promise. We pray: "Jesus, you are the key! Unlock my heart, open my closed doors, and fill my spirit with Mary's courage this day. Amen!"

December 21
Song 2:8–14 or Zeph 3:14–18a; Ps 33:1a, 2–3a,
11–12, 20–21; Lk 1:39–45

O come, O come, O Dayspring from on high.
(Latin hymn, ninth century)

Dawn never happens quickly. Long before dawn, while it is quite dark, the birds start their squawking and singing. Slowly the night changes from dark, to charcoal, to haze, to light. Today's Scripture presents to us the image of waiting. In the gospel, Mary and Elizabeth wait and wonder together. They both were anticipating the dawning of the Lord contained in their wombs. Many times we are called to wait. We must believe that in our waiting also exists the dawning. We believe that the Lord will always draw us from darkness to light. We pray: "Lord, we await your dawning day. Fill our waiting with hints of your light. Amen!"

December 22
1 Sam 1:24–28; 1 Sam 2:1, 4–5, 6–7, 8a; Lk 1:46–56

O come, O come, desire of nations.
(Latin hymn, ninth century)

Have you ever been overcome by the goodness of God? A religious friend told me that he was praying before the shrine of Saint Gerard while on a visit to Italy. A young boy and mother were also at the shrine. He heard the boy say, "Thank you, Saint Gerard." At that point, my friend began to well up with tears and felt overpowered by the love and concern of God. Today's Scripture presents the images of Hannah and Mary, who are both overcome with God's goodness. They desired God, and God gifted them with seeing and bearing the salvation of the nations. We pray: "Lord, let me feel today your overpowering love and goodness. Let me desire to see you like Hannah and Mary. Amen!"

December 23
Mal 3:1–4, 23–24; Ps 25:4–5, 8–9, 10, 14; Lk 1:57–66

O come, O come, Emmanuel.
(Latin hymn, ninth century)

When God is with us (Emmanuel) miracles happen easily and frequently. Children and parents who are estranged turn their hearts to one another as we are shown in the first reading. Zechariah, who is mute, begins to speak and to praise God in today's gospel. This Advent, we invite the miracles of God to happen again in our midst. Like Malachi, we might open our hearts to reconnect with those who are cut off from us. Like Zechariah, we open our mouths to speak words of love and encouragement to those in our families, in our neighborhoods, and in our work communities. We pray: "Jesus, you are 'God with us.' Perform your miracles within me this day that I may speak and live your presence. Amen!"

December 24
2 Sam 7:1–5, 8–11, 16; Ps 89:2–3, 4–5, 26, 28; Lk 1:67–79

I will sing praises to my God all my life long.
(Ps 146:2)

Women during pregnancy share sublime secrets that only other women seem to understand. Mothers, sisters, and girlfriends are members of a sisterhood that gives direction, advice, and understanding during the months of pregnancy and birth. Recently, a friend of mine announced that she and her husband were expecting their first child. I could not help but notice that over the next days and weeks this woman seemed constantly surrounded by other women offering her counsel about the prenatal world.

It is no wonder that Mary in the Gospel sought out her cousin Elizabeth—someone with whom she could share about the glory, goodness, and wonder of God and of her pregnancy. The readings speak about the pregnancy of Mary and how this event establishes a new covenant between God and the chosen people.

Today we also are pregnant with the fullness of the Advent season. It is almost time for us to participate in the birthing of the Lord. We might spend time, like Mary, to understand what this will mean for our lives. We might listen more intently to Scripture to hear the advice and directions that God is giving to us. We might even visit friends who are full of the Advent spirit so we may have fellow travelers in this journey of birth. Let us pray with Mary: "Lord, it is you who are so near birth. Like the stars, the shepherds, and the wise men we wait for you to come again to our world. Renew your peace within us today as we wait. Amen!"

Appendix

Here begins the daily meditations for the additional days of Advent.

Fourth Sunday of Advent

Isa 7:10–14; Ps 24:1–2, 3–4, 5–6; Rom 1:1–7;
Mt 1:18–24 (Cycle A)

2 Sam 7:1–5, 8–11, 14, 16; Ps 89:2–3, 4–5, 27, 29;
Rom 16: 25–27; Lk 1:26–38 (Cycle B)

Mic 5:1–4; Ps 80:2–3, 15–16, 18–19; Heb 10:5–10;
Lk 1: 39–45 (Cycle C)

> *O Key of David, O royal power of Israel,*
> *controlling at your will the gate of heaven:*
> *come, break down the prison walls of death.*
> *(O Antiphon)*

Ahaz refuses to call upon God for a sign. Is that bad? Aren't we taught that to ask God for a sign is, in effect, to admit that we don't completely trust in God's great providence? Of course, God wants to give this sign of fidelity, so the sign is given anyway. Does Ahaz believe?

Joseph doesn't ask for a sign. But Joseph prepares for the coming of the Lord by opening his heart to hear the Word of God. And when the sign is given, Joseph believes its truth.

Paul unreservedly believes the sign he is given on the road to Damascus (Acts 9:3–6), and never looks back. He freely serves as Christ's first and foremost Apostle to the Gentiles, and his loyal and persistent preaching continues to help us realize God's call.

The promise is made to us; the sign is given to us. Today we pray, "Come and save us and free us from our worldly constraints. Open our hearts to receive your Word, for he comes whether we are ready or not. Amen."

[The feast of the Immaculate Conception and the feast of Our Lady of Guadalupe are celebrated during the Advent season. The readings and the reflections that follow are appropriate for your personal celebration of these great feasts of Our Lady. For further reflection refer to Section Twelve, "Family Meal Prayers for the Holiday Season." The prayers provided may be useful.]

December 8
Feast of the Immaculate Conception
Gen 3:9–15, 20; Ps 98:1, 2–3, 3–4; Eph 1:3–6, 11–12; Lk 1:26–38

All the ends of the earth have seen the victory of our God.
(Ps 98:3)

One of the most difficult adult tasks is to make choices. Sometimes our choices are good choices. We find in them peace, love, and future goodness. Sometimes our choices are poor choices and they bring darkness and defeat. Today's readings show us choices. Adam and Eve chose wrongly and that choice opened the door for sin and death. Mary's choice reflected life and goodness and because of her we have been forever blessed. Today we ask God to give us the vision of Mary. Let us make choices today that open the door of life and goodness. We pray: "Lord, give us vision to chose the way of light, life, and godliness, as Mary, my mother, did. Amen!"

December 12
Feast of Our Lady of Guadalupe
Zec 2:14–17 or Rev 11:19, 12:1–6, 10;
Lk 11:26–28 or Lk 1:39–47

My heart exults in the LORD;
my strength is exalted in my God.
(1 Sam 2:1)

Our mother Mary continues to be the forerunner for Jesus. Mary appears to a poor Mexican peasant and asks him to convey her powerful messages to the bishop and to the people. He obeys because, like Mary, his life is a simple "yes" to whatever God would ask. Wealth, massive expectations, or power does not weigh down his peasant life. These readings ask us to return to the days when we were a simple believer. When we could more easily hear God speaking to our spirit. Let us pray for that gift of simplicity on this day: We pray: "Lord, I am your servant. Speak to me! Open my ears that I might hear and my heart that I might obey. Amen."

2. Traditional Meditations of Saint Alphonsus

Saint Alphonsus wrote these meditations around 1750, but because of sickness and other pressing responsibilities he was unable to publish them until much later. Each meditation follows a familiar format popularized by the saint. The theme for meditation is proposed and reflected upon and, at the conclusion of the meditation, affections and prayers are also proposed as an aid to spiritual growth.

Although the reader is free to use these meditations in any way that he or she might find helpful, a quick review of the Alphonsian method of meditation may prove to be helpful.

The method of meditation, as proposed by Saint Alphonsus, consists in three parts: *preparation, consideration,* and *conclusion.* In the *preparation,* we are to remind ourselves of the presence of God and pray a prayer of humility and a prayer of enlightenment. We conclude the preparation segment of our meditation with a Hail Mary to the Blessed Mother and a Glory to the Father in honor of our guardian angel. In the *consideration,* we read the meditation and think about the Passion of Jesus Christ. Saint Alphonsus reminds us that it is important that in the meditation we use our time to produce "affections," prayers of humility, love, sorrow for sin, resignation to the will of God and in making our prayers and petitions known to God. Finally, the *conclusion* is made by praying, "I thank you God for the enlightenment that you have given me; I promise to continue to walk with you in love; and I beg from you the grace to fulfill all that I have promised and hoped for." The saint also strongly recommends concluding the meditation with a prayer for the Poor Souls in Purgatory, which can be found in Section Five, page 89.

Each of the Advent meditations, abridged and edited for today's reader, are meditations of the saint, reflective of the method outlined on the previous page. A meditation is provided for each day of the season; special meditations are provided that is date appropriate beginning on December 16. May they prove to be helpful for your spiritual journey.

First Sunday of Advent

God's goodness is the work of Redemption.

Consider that God, having created the first human being in order that he might serve God and love God in this life and reign with God forever in heaven, enriched humanity with the necessary knowledge and grace. Consider also that ungrateful humanity rebelled against God, refusing God obedience which humanity owed to God in justice and gratitude, and, thus, as miserable sinner, was left with all his posterity a rebel, deprived of divine grace, and forever excluded from paradise. Behold the ruin of humanity caused by sin! All humankind was lost; all were living in blindness or in the shadow of death. The devil had dominion over them and hell destroyed innumerable victims.

But God, seeing all humanity reduced to this miserable state, was moved with pity and resolved to save them. And how was he to accomplish this act of salvation? He was not to send an angel, a seraph, but rather to demonstrate to the world God's immense love, God sent his own son in the likeness of sinful flesh (Rom 8:3).

Consider on the one hand the immense ruin that sin brings upon humanity and consider on the other hand the infinite love, which

God demonstrates, in this great work of the Incarnate Word. How can we do otherwise than exclaim "O infinite goodness! O infinite mercy! O infinite love! God becomes human to die for me!"

First Monday of Advent
Grandeur of the mystery of the Incarnation.

Consider that if God had created a thousand other worlds, a thousand times greater and more beautiful than earth, it is certain that this creation would be infinitely less grand than the Incarnation of the Word. To execute the great work of the Incarnation, all the omnipotence and infinite wisdom of God was necessary in order to unite human nature to the divine Person. In this way, God became a human being; the divinity of the Word became united to the soul and body of Jesus Christ. As a result of this unity, all the actions of the God-Man became divine: his prayers were divine, his steps divine, his sufferings divine, his infant cries divine, his very blood divine, which became, as it were, a fountain of health to wash out all of our sins, and a sacrifice of infinite value.

O holy faith! If faith did not assure us of it, who would be able to believe that a God of infinite majesty would humble himself in order to save humanity, at the cost of so much suffering and disgrace, and of so cruel and shameful death?

O soul, O body, O blood, of my Jesus. I adore you and I thank you. You are my hope. You are the price paid to save me from hell. Listen to my prayers and obtain for me love and perseverance.

First Tuesday of Advent
God's love for humankind.

Consider that the eternal Father, in giving us his son as our Redeemer, could not have given us a stronger motive to love him in return. Saint Augustine teaches that when the Father gave his son there was nothing more that he could give. God desires that we accept this great gift in order to gain eternal salvation, and every other grace that we need. It is in Jesus that we may find all that we truly desire; we find light, strength, peace, confidence, love, and eternal glory; for Jesus Christ is the gift which contains all that we can seek or desire.

God has made the gift of his son a gift to each individual person. As a result of this great gift, each one of us may say: Jesus is all mine; his body is mine; his blood is mine; his life is mine; his sorrows, his death, his merits, are all mine. Every one of us may proclaim, like the apostle Paul, "My Redeemer has loved me, and for the love that he bore me, he has given himself entirely to me."

O God, who could ever have given us this treasure of infinite value but you, a God of infinite love? O my Creator, what more could you have done for me so that I may have confidence in your mercy and your love?

First Wednesday of Advent

The Word was made flesh in the fullness of time.

Consider that God allowed thousands of years to pass, after the sin of Adam and Eve, before he sent his son upon the earth to redeem the world. In the time that passed, the earth was in darkness. The true God was not known or adored, except in one small corner of the earth. Idolatry reigned everywhere so that devils and beasts and stones were adored as gods. But let us pause and admire the divine wisdom. Because the coming of the Redeemer was delayed, the advent of the Redeemer became more welcome. Sin was better known as well as the need of a remedy and the grace of the savior.

This happy time, this advent of the Redeemer which is called the fullness of time, when God sent his son is called the fullness of time on account of the fullness of grace which has been given to us. O happy me! I am now freed from the slavery of Satan and can be governed by the love of my Redeemer. This is what I hope. Help me with your grace so that I may serve you forever, and serve you only for your love.

First Thursday of Advent

The abasement of Jesus.

Consider that the eternal Word descended to the earth to save humankind. Jesus descends from the bosom of his divine Father into the womb of a virgin, a child of Adam and Eve, which in comparison with the bosom of God is an object of horror. In the bosom of the Father the Word is like the Father—immense, omnipotent, most blessed and supreme Lord—but in the womb of Mary he is creature, small, weak, and afflicted.

My beloved Jesus, you are the ruler of heaven and earth, but for my love you made yourself a servant! My sweetest Jesus, permit me never to be separated from you. This grace I ask from you and this grace I will continually pray for until the end of my life. O Mary, my Mother, help me by your intercession that I may never separate myself again from my God.

First Friday of Advent

Jesus enlightens the world and glorifies God.

Consider that before the coming of the Messiah the world was buried in a dark night of ignorance and sin. Everywhere but in Judea sin reigned, a sin which blinds souls and fills them with vices and shields them from understanding that they are enemies of God and condemned. Into this darkness, Jesus came to redeem the world. He delivered the world from idolatry by making known to humankind the light of the true God. He delivered all people from sin by the light of his doctrine and his divine example. He came into the world as an infant at whose birth the angels would sing, "Glory to God in the highest." As a new child, he is the object of the love of all the saints in paradise and gives more glory to God than all the sins of humankind have deprived him of. Let us, therefore, poor sinners, take courage and offer to the Father this infant of love.

O my Father, now that I know the love that you have for me and the patience that you have shown me for so many years, I will no longer live without you. My Father I love you! I love you! I love you!

First Saturday of Advent

The Son of God was laden with all our sins.

Consider the humble state which the Son of God freely chose to assume. He not only took upon himself the form of a slave but also the form of a sinful servant, "in the likeness of sinful flesh." Therefore, Saint Bernard writes, "He not only assumed the form of a servant but even that of a wicked servant." And thus, in this way, he presented himself to his Father, even from his birth, as a criminal and a debtor, guilty of all of our sins, and as such was condemned to die as a malefactor accursed on a cross.

"Behold the man," the Eternal Father seems to say to all of us, showing Jesus to us in the stable of Bethlehem. "This poor child whom you behold, laid in a manger for beasts, and stretched on straw, is my beloved Son, who has come into the world to take upon himself your sins and your sorrows; love him, because he is infinitely worthy of your love and you are under an infinite obligation to do so."

O my innocent Redeemer, enlighten the minds of those who do not know you or who do not love you.

Second Sunday of Advent

God sent the Son to restore us to life.

Consider that sin is the death of the soul, because this enemy of God deprives us of divine grace, which is the life of the soul. Therefore, we miserable sinners, were dead and condemned, but God through the immense love which the Father bears for us, determined to restore us to life. How did he accomplish this? He sent his only-begotten Son into the world to die, so that by his death God might restore us to life.

Behold our Redeemer who has come "so that we might have life to the full." For this purpose, Jesus accepted death so that he might give us life. It is reasonable that we should live only in God. It is reasonable that Jesus should be the only sovereign of our heart since he has spent his blood for us.

O my God! Who would be so ungrateful a wretch as to believe that Jesus died to secure the love of sinful humanity and yet refuse to love him?

Second Monday of Advent

God's Son demonstrates his love in the redemption.

Consider that the eternal Word is so infinitely happy that even the salvation of all humankind could not have added anything to this happiness or diminished it in any way. Consider also that despite this he has nevertheless suffered so much for us—only God is capable of loving to such excess humankind who is so unworthy of being loved.

A devout author once wrote, "If Jesus Christ had permitted us to ask him to give us the greatest proof of his love, who would have asked that he should become a child, that he should clothe himself with all of our miseries, and make himself poor, despised, and ill-treated, even to being put to death by the hands of an executioner, and to be cursed and forsaken by all?"

O my Jesus, I am a poor creature and I was lost through my sins, but you came to save the lost. What, then, should I fear if I am willing to amend my life and become yours?

Second Tuesday of Advent

Jesus, suffering servant in the womb of his mother.

Consider, as the prophet Isaiah once proclaimed, that Jesus is the "suffering servant" and from his infancy began to endure the greatest sorrows. Even from the womb of Mary, Jesus Christ accepted obediently the will of his Father. He foresaw the scourges, the thorns, the blows, the nails, and the cross on which he offered his life. He suffered a continual martyrdom and he offered every moment for us to his eternal Father. But what afflicted him more than any other suffering was the malice of every sin, when he saw the immense number that would be committed.

My sweetest Redeemer, when shall I begin to be grateful to you for your infinite goodness? When shall I begin to acknowledge the love that you have for me and the sorrows that you endured for me? Shall I continue to live an ungrateful life? No, my Jesus, by the help of your grace, it shall not be so.

Second Wednesday of Advent

Jesus is charged with the sins of the whole world.

Consider that the divine Word, in taking on the human form, chose not only to take the form of a sinner but also to bear the sins of all humanity. What must have been the anguish of the heart of the infant Jesus when he discovered that divine justice insisted that he make full satisfaction for each sin! Our Lord once showed to Saint Catherine of Siena the hideousness of one single venial sin, and such was the dread and sorrow of the saint that she fell senseless to the ground. What, then, must have been the suffering of the infant Jesus when he saw before him the immense array of all the crimes of humanity?

My beloved Jesus, I who have offended you am not worthy of your favors. Help me, O Lord, to make that act of contrition, which I now intend to do. You do not deserve to be offended, my Jesus, but rather to be loved. My blessed Redeemer, help me.

Second Thursday of Advent
Jesus suffers during his whole life.

Consider that all the sufferings that Jesus endured in his life and death were all present to him from the first moment of his life. Consider that even from his childhood he began to offer them to fulfill his role as our Redeemer. What martyrdom did the loving heart of Jesus constantly endure in beholding all the sins of humankind! Saint Thomas says that the sorrow which Jesus felt at the knowledge of the injury done to his Father, and of the evil that sin would cause to the souls that he loved, surpassed the sorrow of all contrite sinners that ever existed.

Saint Margaret of Cortona never ceased to shed tears for her sins. One day her confessor said to her, "No more tears, Margaret, it is enough, our Lord has already forgiven you." "What," answered the saint, "how can my tears and my sorrows suffice for the sins which my Jesus was afflicted all his life long?"

My beloved Redeemer, I thank you. I could die of sorrow when I think of how I have abused your infinite goodness. Forgive me, my Love, and come and take entire possession of my heart.

Second Friday of Advent

Jesus suffers so much in order to gain our hearts.

Consider that Jesus suffered for our love. During his entire life, he had no other purpose than the glory of God and our salvation. Even though he could have saved us without suffering, he chose to embrace a life of suffering. He was poor, despised, and deprived of every comfort, with a death that was more desolate and bitter than any death ever endured by a martyr or penitent. All of this was done for the sole purpose of helping us understand the greatness of his love for us.

Saint Bonaventure exclaims, "It is a wonder to see a God endure such sufferings, shedding tears in a stable, poor in a workshop, languishing on a cross, in short, afflicted and troubled his whole life, all because of his love for sinful humanity."

O sovereign God, help me not to be ungrateful for all that you have given me. Help me to die in love with you. Mary, my hope, help me. Pray to Jesus for me.

Second Saturday of Advent

The greatest sorrow of Jesus.

Consider Jesus, who revealed to the Venerable Agatha of the Cross, that which afflicted him more than any other sorrow was hardness of the hearts of humanity. This sorrow was the bitter chalice that Jesus begged the Father to remove from him, saying, "Let this chalice pass from me." What chalice? The contempt with which his love was treated. Our Lord revealed to Saint Catherine of Siena that this was the reason that he exclaimed from the cross, "My God, my God, why have you forsaken me?"

Knowing this sorrow, let us change our will, repent of our sins, and resolve to love God. In this way, we shall then find peace, that is, the divine friendship that we seek. We beg the Lord for the necessary grace to execute what we propose. We call upon our Blessed Lady and ask that she not cease to pray until we are changed and made into what God wishes us to be.

O my most amiable Jesus, how much have I caused you to suffer? In the future, I will love you above all other things, ready to give up my life a thousand times in order to accomplish your will.

Third Sunday of Advent

The poverty of the infant Jesus

Consider that in order to contemplate with tenderness and love the birth of Jesus, we must pray to the Lord to a give us a lively faith. If we enter the grotto in Bethlehem without faith, we shall have nothing but a feeling of compassion as we view an infant, in the depth of winter, laid in a manger in the midst of a cold cavern. However, if we enter with faith, and consider the kind of love that would prompt God to humble himself in this way, we would feel compelled to give all our affection and love to this infant God. Saint Luke says that the shepherds, after visiting Jesus in the manger, "returned to their flocks glorifying and praising God for all that they had heard and experienced."

O my amiable and sweet infant Jesus, although I see you so poor and lying on straw, I nevertheless adore and worship you as my Lord. I love you, my infant Savior; I love you, my infant God; I love you, my love, my life, and my all.

Third Monday of Advent

Jesus is the fountain of grace.

Consider the four fountains of grace that we have in Jesus, as contemplated by Saint Bernard. The first fountain is the mercy fountain, from which we may wash ourselves clean from the filthiness of our sins. The second fountain is the fountain of peace and consolation, from which we may drink deeply in our experience of trials and tribulations. The third fountain is that of devotion, in which we will be strengthened to follow the divine will of God. The fourth fountain is the fountain of love, that fountain in which we are inflamed by the love of God and in which we experience the blessed fire that Jesus came upon the earth to enkindle. How true it is that the person who drinks deeply from these fountains will be blessed and will draw from them waters of joy and of salvation.

O my most sweet and dearest Savior, how much do I owe you? You have loved me and yet I have not loved you with all of my affection and desire. Help me to esteem your grace above all other things. My dear Mother Mary, help me obtain the necessary grace to live and die loving Jesus.

Third Tuesday of Advent

Jesus is the loving physician of our souls.

Consider, as Saint Augustine says, "Jesus descends to the bed of the sick," that is to say that Jesus, has taken upon himself our flesh, the body which is the bed of the infirm soul. Consider also that Jesus, in order to cure our infirmity, has taken upon himself our flesh. Most other physicians would use all of their efforts to cure the sick, but what physician would take upon themselves the infirmity of their patient? Jesus Christ is the physician who has assumed our infirmities in order to cure us. He has not sent another in his place, but has chosen to suffer in this way in order to win our love. He chose to heal our wounds with his own blood, and by his death, deliver us from death and to obtain for us everlasting life.

O my Redeemer, be forever praised and blessed! What would become of my soul, infirmed and afflicted with the many sores of my sins, if you had not been willing to heal me? O blood of my savior, I trust in you, wash me and cure me.

Third Wednesday of Advent

We should hope for all things because of the merits of Jesus Christ.

Consider that since the eternal Father has given us his own Son to be our mediator and advocate, and the victim of satisfaction for our sins, that we should not despair of obtaining from God whatever we may desire. Although it is true that none of our prayers deserve to be heard or granted and we deserve punishment for our sins, it is also true that Jesus intercedes for us and offers us his life, his blood, and his death. Jesus deserves to be heard and the Father cannot refuse anything to so dear a Son. Let us, therefore, thank God and hope for all things from the merits of Jesus Christ.

Eternal Father, for the love of Jesus Christ, give me light and strength to accomplish your holy will. I trust in the merits of Jesus Christ, and I hope that you will answer my prayer.

December 16

God has given his only Son to save us.

Consider that the eternal Father has given his Son to the world for the light and life of all people in order that he might win salvation. Consider also that the Father, in sending his Son to be our Redeemer and Mediator has, in a certain sense, bound himself to forgive us and love us. On the other hand, the divine Word, having accepted the invitation of his Father, has also bound himself to love us; not for our own merits but rather to fulfill the merciful will of his Father.

O infinite God, and only love of my soul, I thank you, for having given me your Son. For the sake of this same Son, accept me, and bind me with chains of love to my Redeemer.

December 17

The heart of Jesus in the womb of his mother.

Consider that whatever Jesus suffered in his life and in his passion was all placed before him while he was in the womb of Mary. He accepted everything that was proposed to him with delight, but in accepting all things, and in overcoming the natural repugnance of sense, O my God, what anguish and oppression did the innocent heart of Jesus suffer. Our Redeemer accepted each moment even though he continually had before his eyes that confusion which he would one day feel at seeing himself stripped naked, scourged, and suspended by three iron nails, ending his life in the midst of insults and curses. And for what? To save us miserable and ungrateful sinners.

My beloved Redeemer, how much did it cost you to raise me from the ruin, which I brought on myself through my sins? What can I do without your grace? I can do nothing but pray that you will help me, but even this prayer comes from the merits of your suffering and death. O my Jesus, help me.

December 18

Jesus made himself a child to gain our confidence and our love.

Consider that the Son of God has made himself little in order to make us great. He has given himself to us, that we might give ourselves to him. He has come to show us his love, that we may respond to it by giving him ours. Let us, therefore, receive him with affection, let us love him, and call upon him with all our needs.

"A child gives easily," says Saint Bernard. Children readily give whatever is asked of them. Jesus came into the world as a child to demonstrate that he was ready and willing to give all. If we wish for light, Jesus has come to enlighten us. If we desire strength, he will strengthen us. If we wish for pardon, he has come to pardon us. In short, he has come to give us all that we need.

O my Jesus, you have descended from heaven to give yourself entirely to us. How can we turn our backs on you? I have been loved by you and I have also been ungrateful. O my Redeemer, forgive the injuries that I have committed against you.

December 19

The passion of Jesus lasted throughout his whole life.

Consider that when Abraham was leading his son Isaac to death that he did not give him notice of it beforehand, even during the short time that was necessary for them to arrive at the mount. But the eternal Father chose that his incarnate Son, whom he had destined to be the victim for the atonement of our sins, should know the sorrow he was to endure from the very first moment that he was in his mother's womb. The whole life, then, of our blessed Redeemer, and all the years that he spent, was a life of pain and tears. His divine heart never passed one moment free from suffering. The martyrs have suffered, but assisted by grace, they suffered with joy and fervor. Jesus Christ suffered, but he suffered with a heart full of weariness and sorrow, and he accepted all for our love.

O sweet, O amiable, O loving heart of Jesus, I thank you. O afflicted and loving heart of my Lord, I thank you for all that you suffered for me.

December 20

Jesus offered himself for our salvation from the beginning.

Consider that the divine Word knew that all the sacrifices of goats and bulls offered to the Father in times past had not been able to satisfy for the sins of humankind, but that it required a divine person to pay the price of redemption. "My Father," said Jesus, "all the victims previously offered to you have not paid the debt, nor could they have paid the debt, necessary to satisfy your justice. You have given me my humanity, in order that by shedding my blood, I might please you and save humanity. Behold I come. Here I am. I am ready. I accept everything, and I submit myself in everything to your will."

O my Jesus, I am weak, grant me strength against temptation. I am infirm, I hope that your precious blood will be my medicine. I am a sinner, but I hope that your grace will make me a saint. I acknowledge that I have cooperated with my own ruin, but this day I promise always to call upon you, and in this way cooperate with your grace.

December 21

Jesus is a prisoner in the womb of Mary.

Consider the painful life that Jesus Christ led in the womb of his mother, and the long-confined and dark imprisonment that he suffered there for nine months. He had his senses, but he could not use them. A tongue, but he could not speak. Eyes, but he could not see. Hands, but he could not stretch them out. Feet, but he could not walk. For nine months he had to remain in the womb of Mary, a voluntary prison but also a prison of love. He was innocent, but he had offered himself to make payment for our debts and our crimes. What gratitude and love we should demonstrate for our Lord in return for the love and goodness that he has given to us. He has put himself into chains in order to deliver us from the chains of hell.

O my Jesus, you are the innocent one. I implore you to bind my poor soul to your feet by your holy love, so that it may never again be separated from you.

December 22

The sorrow that the ingratitude of humankind has caused Jesus.

Consider that Saint Francis of Assisi, during the days of the holy Nativity, went about the highways and woods with sighs and tears and inconsolable lamentations. When asked the reason he responded, "Why should I not weep when I see that love is not loved! I see a God who became human for the love of humanity, and humanity that is ungrateful to this God." Now, if this ingratitude caused so much sorrow in the heart of Saint Francis, consider how much more it must have afflicted the heart of Jesus Christ. The loving infant does not deserve this response. He came from heaven to suffer and die for us, so that we might love him. How can we remain ungrateful?

O my Jesus, I love you, and will always love you. Inflame my heart every day with the memory of your love for me. Mary, my mother, help me to live a life grateful to God who has loved me, even after I have so greatly offended him.

December 23

God's love is demonstrated by the birth of Jesus.

Consider the love of God. It was always present but did not always appear. It was first promised in many prophecies and foreshadowed by many figures, but at the birth of our Redeemer, this divine love did indeed appear. But despite the birth of Jesus, why is it that so many people have not known God's love and so many people seem ignorant of his love? This is the reason, "The light of the world has come into the world, and humanity loves darkness rather than the light." They have not known him, and they do not know him, because they do not wish to know him, loving rather the darkness of sin than the light of grace. Let each one determine this day not to be numbered among those unhappy souls who prefer the darkness.

O my holy Infant, now I see you lying on the straw, poor, afflicted, and forsaken. I have been one of those ungrateful ones who do not know you. Help me never to forget you again.

December 24

Saint Joseph goes to Bethlehem with his holy spouse.

Consider that God had decreed that his Son be born, not in Joseph's house, but in a cavern and stable of beasts, in the poorest and most painful way a child can be born. For this reason God caused Caesar to publish an edict, by which people were commanded to go and register each member of their family, in their place of origin. When Joseph heard this order he was agitated and unsure whether or not the Virgin Mother should take the trip with him. But Mary, knowing of his dilemma and being well versed in the prophet Micheas responded, "Do not fear, I will go with you and the Lord will assist us." She then gathered together the swaddling clothes and the other miserable garments already prepared for the journey and departed with Joseph. Let us accompany Mary and Joseph on their journey and await the appearance of the King of Heaven.

My beloved Redeemer, I know that in this journey the angels in heaven accompanied you, but I also wish to accompany you, O my only love. My soul has become filled with love for you, O my amiable infant God. Unite and bind me to yourself.

Saints and Feast Days of the Advent Season

The liturgical calendar between the feast of the apostle Andrew and the feast of the Epiphany is a microcosm of the liturgical year. In this short time, the Church celebrates the memory of apostles and evangelists, major feast days of the Blessed Mother, and a variety of saints, both men and women, from across the spectrum. This liturgical season provides us with a snapshot, a quick view, of some of the dogmas and the doctrines that are central to Christianity. The season also celebrates some of the people who have made those same dogmas and doctrines living—the people represented here have breathed the life of faith and the life of humanity into the creedal formulations of the season.

In addition to a short exposition of the life of the saint or the meaning of the feast day celebrated, a traditional prayer, appropriate for the day, is often provided. Every attempt was made to discover the most traditional prayer or expression of devotion available. The older prayers seem to possess a different emphasis and flavor, not universally present in the newer liturgical adaptations. The traditional expression of piety and devotion capture a sense of the reason why the particular saint or feast day remained important in the piety of the people.

1. Saint Andrew, Apostle (November 30)

Andrew, the brother of Simon Peter, was one of the first disciples called by the Lord. A fisherman, from Bethsaida in Galilee, Andrew (as we learn in the Gospel of John) was a disciple of John the Baptist. In the Gospel of Mark (1:16), we learn that Jesus called Andrew while he was fishing with his brother. His name appears two other times, (both references are found in the Gospel of John)—once when he calls attention to the young boy who has some loaves and some fish (6:8) and then when some people approach the apostles requesting an opportunity to see Jesus (12:22).

Tradition tells us that after the death of Jesus he preached the gospel in Scythia and in Greece. There is also some indication that he preached in Byzantium. And, finally, a very old tradition records the circumstances of his death; he was crucified on an X-shaped cross in southern Greece. Saint Andrew is the patron Saint of Russia and of Scotland.

PRAYER TO ANDREW

Andrew, first called of the apostles and brother of Peter their leader, intercede with the Master of All that he may grant peace to the world and great mercy to our souls. Amen.

2. Saint Francis Xavier, Priest (December 3)

Saint Francis was born on April 7, 1506, at the family castle near Pamplona in the Basque area of Spain. A member of the landed nobility, he had many opportunities presented to him, one of which was the opportunity to pursue higher education at the University of Paris. It was at the university that he met Saint Ignatius of Loyola, the founder of the Jesuits. He disagreed with many of the ideas presented by Saint Ignatius, but he eventually determined to set aside his differences. He became one of the first seven Jesuits who took their vows in 1534. He was ordained in 1537 in Venice with Saint Ignatius and four others. On his thirty-fifth birthday, April 7, 1541, he left for the Far East, visiting the East Indies, India, New Guinea, Morotai (very near to the Philippines), and Japan, to a name only a few of the places where his missionary activity took him. In each place, he converted thousands of people, primarily through the use of interpreters, which made his preaching all the more remarkable. His life was marked by intense missionary activity, hardship, very little cooperation and very little funding, but always present was the good example and witness of his own life which people found both endearing and inspiring. His dream was to travel to China, but he died on December 3, 1552, in sight of his goal but just out of reach.

Many people consider him to be the greatest Christian missionary since the apostle Paul.

Saint Francis Xavier is known at the Apostle of the Indies and the Apostle of Japan. Pope Pius X proclaimed him the patron of all foreign missionaries.

NOVENA PRAYER TO SAINT FRANCIS XAVIER

O great Saint Francis, well beloved and full of charity, I reverently join you in the adoration of the divine Majesty. Since I rejoice in the singular gifts of grace that were given to you in life and of glory after death, I give thanks to God and beg you, with all the affections of my heart, for your powerful intercession. I ask that you obtain for me above all things the grace to live a holy life and die a holy death. Moreover I beg you to obtain for me *(here insert some special spiritual or temporal favor)*, but if what I ask does not contribute to the glory of God and the greater good of my soul, obtain for me that which will more certainly accomplish this end. Amen.

3. Saint John Damascene, Priest and Doctor (December 4)

Saint John was born into a wealthy Christian family at Damascus, Syria, in the year 675. He spent his entire life under Islamic rule and served in the government of Caliph Abdul Malek as chief revenue officer, a position that his father had held before him. Educated by a brilliant monk named Cosmas, a slave in his families household, he proved himself to be a capable student and an original thinker. In 726, he resigned his government position and became a monk at the Monastery of Saint Sabas outside of Jerusalem. While in Jerusalem, he became embroiled in a controversy concerning the proper use and veneration of sacred images. He boldly defended the Catholic position and also contributed many different hymns and canons that are still used today in Byzantine liturgies. Because of the elegance of his Greek, he is often identified as Chrysorrhoas, or "gold pouring."

Saint John died on December 5, in the year 749. The last of the Greek Fathers of the Church, Pope Leo XIII proclaimed John a Doctor of the Church in 1890.

PRAYER TO SAINT JOHN DAMASCENE

Guide and mirror of piety and exemplary behavior, bright star of the universe and adornment of pontiffs, you enlightened us all by your teachings. O wise John, inspired by God and lyre of the Holy Spirit, intercede with Christ God that He may save our souls! Amen.

4. Saint Nicholas, Bishop (December 6)

Very little is known about Saint Nicholas. We know that he was born of wealthy parents in Asia Minor and that he was named bishop of the Diocese of Myra in Lycia (now part of Turkey). We also know that he died in 350. Other than these meager facts, everything else that we know about Saint Nicholas comes from the stories and the legends that are associated with him. However, each of these stories speaks about a man who was generous and kind above all else. Perhaps the legend that is the most popular is the story that tells about him saving three young girls from a life of prostitution. According to the story, the girls' father was forced to sell them because he had no way of providing the dowry that was required of them in order to be married. Saint Nicholas, on hearing of their plight, threw three bags of gold through the window of the father's house, providing the much-needed dowries and saving the girls from a life of misery. This legend gave rise to the custom of young girls' giving presents to members of their families in his honor, which somehow led to the eventual custom of the giving of gifts at Christmas. Although Saint Nicholas is often associated with Santa Claus, there is no direct linkage that would explain this association.

Regardless, the association is there, as are the practices and the customs of the feast of Christmas and the holiday season. Saint Nicholas is the patron saint of Greece and Sicily and is also one of the patron saints of Russia.

Glorious Saint Nicholas, my special patron, from your throne in glory where you enjoy the presence of God, turn your eyes in pity upon me and obtain for me from our Lord the graces and helps that I need in my spiritual and temporal necessities (*and especially this favor, provided that it is profitable to my eternal salvation*). Be mindful, likewise, O glorious and saintly bishop, of our sovereign Pontiff, of the Holy Church, and of all Christian people. Bring back to the way of salvation all those who are living steeped in sin and blinded by the darkness of ignorance, error, and heresy. Comfort the afflicted, provide for the needy, strengthen the fearful, defend the oppressed, and give health to the infirm. Cause all people to experience the effects of your powerful intercession with the supreme Giver of every good and perfect gift. Amen.

5. Saint Ambrose, Bishop and Doctor (December 7)

Saint Ambrose (340–397) was born in Trier, Germany, where his father was a high official in the Roman government. After his father's death, he returned to Rome and was educated there. At the age of thirty, after successfully completing his studies and beginning the practice of law, he was appointed the governor of the Milan Province. In Milan, attracted to the Christian faith, he became a catechumen, preparing for his baptism. While still a catechumen, he attended the gathering of the local church community as they discerned candidates for the office of Bishop of Milan. He intervened in the election process because there was so much friction between two opposing factions. The people were so impressed with his abilities and his leadership that they immediately accepted it as the will of God when a young boy called out, "Let Ambrose be the one selected!" He was baptized, and much against his will, was ordained as the bishop after the emperor confirmed his selection (the custom of the time).

Once Ambrose was selected as bishop, he dedicated himself completely to the ministry of the Church, devoting his considerable talents to the challenges that faced the community. He was an excellent preacher (Saint Augustine heard him preach, and the sermon became a catalyst for his own conversion), well versed in Scripture, and an expert on the principles regarding the relationship between the Church and the state, principles that are still applied today. He was a much sought-after consultor to the emperors and a mediator in numerous disputes. He was well respected and loved. After his death he was canonized and proclaimed a Doctor of the Church.

PRAYER TO SAINT AMBROSE

Through your knowledge of the things of God, you nourish the minds of the faithful, O wise Father Ambrose. The graces you obtain for us constantly yield spiritual fruits for us, and through your abundant healing power, you cleanse all our human passions. You are a seer full of divine wisdom, Holy Ambrose. Amen.

6. Feast of the Immaculate Conception (December 8)

In 1854, Pope Pius IX formally declared the Immaculate Conception of Mary to be an official teaching of the Church. Four years later, on March 25 in the grotto at Lourdes, France, the young peasant girl Bernadette Soubirous, asked the Lady who had appeared to her to reveal who she was. The Lady responded, "I am the Immaculate Conception."

The Immaculate Conception (Mary's own beginnings in the womb of her mother, Saint Anne) is a mystery of faith, often misunderstood, and more often than not, confused (with the virgin birth of Jesus). The meaning of the dogma is that Mary received the singular and glorious privilege of being truly "filled with grace," because she had been chosen to bear Jesus in her womb. Because she had been chosen to bear Jesus in her womb, her redemption began at the moment of her conception.

As Pope John Paul II has often pointed out, all of humanity participates in redemption through the mystery of grace, which is a sharing in God's interior life. However, the Blessed Mother, because she was preserved from sin by the direct intervention of God, demonstrates to us that all people can be in fact freed from sin and the effects of sin. Our deliverance comes after our birth through the sacrament of baptism. Even if lost later through sin, our redemption can be recaptured through reconciliation. What happened to our Blessed Mother and what happens to us both reflect God's overwhelming and gracious love for us.

IMMACULATE CONCEPTION PRAYER

O Virgin Immaculate, who was pleasing in the sight of the Lord and did become his mother, look graciously upon the wretched who implore your mighty patronage. The wicked serpent, against whom the primal curse was hurled, continues none the less to wage war and to lay snares for the unhappy children of Eve. O Blessed Mother, our Queen and Advocate, who from the first moment of your conception crushed the head of our enemy, receive the prayers that we unite single-heartedly to you so that you may offer them at the throne of God, that we may never fall into the snares that are laid for us. May we all come to the haven of salvation, and, in the midst of so many dangers, may the holy Church and the fellowship of Christians everywhere sing once more the hymn of deliverance, victory, and peace. Amen.

7. Saint Damasus I, Pope (December 11)

Of Spanish descent, Damasus (305–384) was born in Rome. His father was a priest, and he became a deacon in his father's church. Little is known of his life and his work until the year 366 when, at the age of sixty-one, he was elected Bishop of Rome in a bitterly contested election. For the entire eighteen years that he served as bishop, it was necessary to combat the factions that opposed him. This opposition group even went so far as to elect an anti-pope, and it was only after the direct intervention of the emperor that Damasus's election was secure.

As Bishop of Rome, he devoted his energies to strengthening the office and the influence of the papacy, combating heresy, and promoting the study of Scripture. His efforts of persuasion were instrumental in convincing Saint Jerome, who served as his personal secretary, to begin work on the Vulgate translation of the Bible. Damasus had a special love of and devotion to the martyrs, and it was through his efforts that catacombs, shrines, and tombs of the martyrs became regular place for pilgrimage and devotion. He was pope when, in 380, the emperors of the East and the West declared Christianity the official religion of the Roman Empire.

PRAYER TO SAINT DAMASUS I

Holy Damasus, you who served as pope during a troubled period of the Church's history, give us the wisdom to reconcile opposing forces yet remain loyal to the underlying truth. As the mentor of Saint Jerome and commissioner of the revised Latin translation of the New Testament, as the restorer of the catacombs and the tombs of the martyrs, grant us the foresight to always foster what is best for our family and friends. Amen.

8. Saint Jane Frances de Chantal, Religious (December 12)

Jane was born in Dijon, France, on January 23, 1572. She was not, as were so many other saints, born of humble origins, but rather she was the daughter of a rich and prominent politician. She married and was the mother four children, but her husband died a tragic death after only seven years of marriage. After his death, Jane intended to simply take care of her children, but she met a very remarkable man who completely changed her life. In 1604, when Jane was thirty-two years old she met Bishop Francis de Sales. Together they were determined to found a new religious order for women, the Order of the Visitation, whose members were called to imitate the Blessed Mother, especially her virtues of caring for the poor and the sick. The order proved to be very popular and by the time of her death, at the age of sixty-nine on December 13, 1641, eighty Visitation convents were in existence. Although Francis de Sales had died twenty years earlier, his friend and fellow saint, Vincent de Paul, had become her guide. It was Vincent de Paul who paid her the final tribute: "I regard her as one of the holiest souls I have ever met on this earth."

Pope Clement XIII canonized Saint Jane Frances de Chantal on July 16, 1767. Saint Francis de Sales wrote his great spiritual classic *On the Love of God* in her honor.

PRAYER TO SAINT JANE FRANCES DE CHANTAL

Holy Saint Jane, under the guidance of Saint Francis de Sales, you surrendered your life to God's love and will. Like you, I thank God for those persons in my life who support me on my spiritual journeys. Pray that the Spirit of Wisdom and Love be with all of my companions, that they may support and love me as I need. Amen.

9. Feast of Our Lady of Guadalupe (December 12)
(North and South America)

On December 9, 1521, ten years after the conquest of Mexico by the Spanish, the Blessed Virgin Mary appeared to Juan Diego, a native Indian, with instructions that a church be built to her on that very spot. When Juan Diego went to tell the bishop of this apparition, he requested a sign from Our Lady so that he might be believed. The Blessed Virgin asked him to pick some roses at the place of the apparition (a desolate rocky place that was not the usual place where roses might grow). Juan Diego filled his cloak with roses and went to see the bishop, and as he unrolled his cloak to show the roses to the bishop, the image of the Blessed Virgin of Guadalupe was imprinted on his cloak. In this image, the Blessed Mother was portrayed, not as a noble Spanish lady, but rather as a native Indian woman, in the traditional dress of the time. A small adobe chapel was erected at the site of the apparitions, probably around 1531, and later a larger basilica was built on the spot.

PRAYER TO OUR LADY OF GUADALUPE

Beautiful Lady of Tepeyac Hill, clothed in rays of sunshine bright, softly etched on a peasant's cloak, your radiant beauty brings delight. Not to the Fathers did you appear, nor to bishops in hallowed hall. To a people oppressed, you turn your face; to a race despised, you call. From these people you chose a son Juan Diego, suffering servant. As roses blossomed in rocky soil, out of season, out of place, So did hearts frozen in hatred melt, and so did radiant faith take root. Virgin Mother of our God, soften our hearts and fill them now; call us out of our narrowness; challenge us in our shallowness, and bring us into your Son's embrace. Amen.

10. Saint Lucy, Virgin and Martyr (December 13)

Except for legends, little is known of Saint Lucy, one of the early virgin martyrs. (This same dearth of information also applies to Agnes, Cecilia, Agatha, and Anastasia, all of whom are mentioned in the Roman Canon, Canon Number One, of the Mass.) According to tradition, Lucy was born in Sicily, and when she refused marriage, she was denounced for her Christian beliefs, and sentenced to a brothel. Even in the brothel her enemies were unable to prevail against her. She was sentenced to be burned at the stake, but the flames did not harm her. Finally, in frustration, the guards stabbed her to death through her throat. Those who have eye trouble, perhaps because her name means "light," often invoke Saint Lucy.

PRAYER TO SAINT LUCY

O glorious virgin and martyr, Saint Lucy, we behold with wonder the light of living faith, which the God of mercy was pleased to infuse into your fair soul. By the light of this faith, you were enabled to despise the vain and fleeting things of this miserable world and to keep your eyes fixed on heaven, for which alone we have been created. Your spirit was not darkened nor your heart ensnared by the honors, riches, and pleasures offered to you by a deceitful world to the loss of faith and the grace of God. Far from yielding to the wicked proposals of the impious Prefect, you showed yourself to be brave and resolute even to death itself, rather than prove unfaithful to the heavenly Master. How great ought to be our shame who have been illuminated by the same faith and fortified by the grace of God, and are nevertheless unable to resist our guilty passions or to despise the crooked maxims of the world, or to turn a deaf ear to the cunning suggestions of our hellish foe. Dear saint, obtain for us more light from almighty God to enable us to see clearly the great truth that we are not made for things below but for unseen things above. Amen.

11. Saint John of the Cross, Priest and Doctor (December 14)

Saint John of the Cross was born Juan de Yepes on June 24, 1542, in the small Spanish city of Fontiveras. He died forty-nine years later on December 14, 1591, in the equally small city of Ubeda. His short time on earth was spent in a taunt circle (scarcely more than a hundred miles in diameter) of towns and villages, mostly located in the Castillean region of Spain. Yet his influence on the prayer life of those seeking closer union with God has been worldwide. His own prayer life was influenced by two important events: his entrance into the Carmelites and his friendship with Saint Teresa of Ávila, called by some the "greatest woman on the earth." He was a brilliant student, a priest, a man interested in the mystical writings of his time, and a man who determined that prayer and penance would be the predominant factors in his life. He is the author of the spiritual classics *Dark Night of the Soul, Living Flame of Love, Ascent of Mount Carmel* and *The Spiritual Canticle.*

John spent the last years of his life in solitude and prayer. His death came suddenly and was, as he had hoped, hardly noticed. However, after his death, his reputation for holiness grew. Pope Benedict XIII declared him a saint in 1726, and in 1926 he was declared a Doctor of the Church.

PRAYER TO SAINT JOHN OF THE CROSS

O glorious Saint John who, through a pure desire of being like Jesus crucified, did long for nothing up to the moment of your last breath, than to be despised and to be made little of by all, and whose thirst after sufferings was so burning that your noble heart rejoiced in the midst of the worst torments and afflictions, I beg you, dear saint, by the glory which your many sufferings have gained for you, to intercede for me, and obtain for me of God a love of suffering, together with the grace and strength to bear with firmness all trials and adversities, which are the sure means to the happy attainment of that glorious crown which awaits me in heaven. Dear saint, from your most happy throne of glory, where you are now seated in majesty, hear, I beg you, my prayers, so that, after your example, full of love for the cross and for suffering, I may deserve to be your companion in glory. Amen.

12. Saint Peter Canisius, Priest and Doctor (December 21)

Saint Peter (1521–1597) was born in the Netherlands of a very wealthy family. He entered the Society of Jesus (the Jesuits) after completing his studies at the universities in Cologne and Louvain and gave his substantial inheritance to the poor. He was ordained a priest in 1546 and was assigned to teach. However, his reputation as a convincing and effective preacher became well known, and Duke William of Bavaria requested that he be transferred to Germany in order to help in the revival of Catholicism. While in Bavaria, he effectively defended the Catholic faith, preached the dogmas and doctrines of the Church as defined by the Council of Trent, and established many colleges and seminaries known for their orthodoxy and excellence. His influence was widespread and long lasting.

Of the many projects and efforts that he engaged in, perhaps the single most effective was his catechism which was eventually translated into fifteen languages. His *Manual of Catholics* was also very popular. Saint Peter was known as the "second apostle of Germany," after the great Saint Boniface, and he can certainly be credited with reestablishing Catholicism in southern Germany after the Reformation.

Near the end of his life, Saint Peter suffered a stroke which severely disabled him. However he did not stop writing and he continued to be an effective force for evangelization. He was canonized in 1925 and declared a Doctor of the Church.

Saint Peter Canisius, you saw the good in even the most trouble-some of people. You found their talents and used them. Help me to see beyond the behavior of others that may bother me to the gifts God has given them. Amen.

13. Saint John of Kanty, Priest (December 23)

Also known as John Cantius (1390–1473), he was born in Kanti, Po-land, and became a priest of the Diocese of Cracow. A brilliant Scrip-ture scholar, he taught for many years at the University of Cracow until certain jealous members of the faculty succeeded in hounding him out of the university. He became a parish priest at Olkusz but was not very effective in his ministry. Indications of scrupulosity made it very difficult for John to devote himself to the care of souls. He returned to Cracow and resumed teaching until his death. He was known for his scholarship and learning, but also for his personal simplicity of life and his love and care for the poor. He was canon-ized in 1767 and declared the patron of Poland and Lithuania.

PRAYER TO SAINT JOHN OF KANTY

Blessed Saint John of Cantius, instill in us the devotion to the poor which you courageously exhibited in your life and foster in us a spirit of detachment from worldly concerns. Amen.

14. Saint Stephen, First Martyr (December 26)

Stephen, in Greek the name means "crown," was the first martyr of the Christian faith. The story of his martyrdom may be found in the Acts of the Apostles, chapters 6 and 7. His death is remarkable be-cause, while the crowd was stoning him to death, he prayed that his soul might be received into heaven and that his slayers would be immediately forgiven. According to Scripture, devout men, "bewailing him loudly as they did so" buried Stephen's broken body. What is more to the point is his positive witness (the word *martyr* means "witness"), and the fact that his death marked the beginning of a series of persecutions. Another remarkable point about his death was that Saul, later to become the great Apostle to the Gentiles, witnessed it.

An ancient preacher painted a picture of Stephen and the apostle Paul together in heaven with these words, "Paul rejoices with Stephen, exults, delights, reigns with Stephen. Stephen went first, slain by the stones thrown by Paul, but Paul followed after, helped by the prayers of Stephen. Paul feels no shame because of Stephen's death, and Stephen delights in Paul's companionship, for love fills them both with joy. Stephen's love prevailed over the cruelty of the mob. Paul's love covered the multitude of sins. It was the love that won for both of them the kingdom of heaven."

PRAYER TO SAINT STEPHEN, PROTOMARTYR

The apostles chose Stephen the deacon, a man full of faith and the Holy Spirit, who was stoned while he prayed, saying "Lord Jesus, receive my spirit, and lay not this sin upon them."

V. By the merits and prayers of blessed Stephen,

R. Be merciful, O God, to your people.

Let us pray. Almighty and everlasting God, who consecrated the first-fruits of your martyrs in the blood of the blessed Stephen the deacon; grant, we beg you, that he may pray for us, even as he prayed for his persecutors, to our Lord Jesus Christ your son, who lives and reigns world without end. Amen.

15. Saint John, Apostle and Evangelist (December 27)

John the Evangelist, also known as John the Divine, because of his theological brilliance, was probably born around the year 6 in Galilee, the son of Zebede and Salome, the younger brother of James the Greater. He was a fisherman, called by Jesus, and was the youngest apostle. All indications were that he was "beloved of Jesus," and very close to the Lord, present at all of the most important moments (the Transfiguration, Crucifixion, and a witness to the empty tomb of the Resurrection). After the death of Jesus, he became a missionary, traveling to Asia Minor and to Rome, but he was also present at the Church in Jerusalem and identified by the apostle Paul as a leader and a pillar of the Jerusalem church. Tradition places him at the death of the Blessed Mother.

John is best known as an evangelist, the author of the fourth gospel, the book of Revelation, and three different epistles. However, there is no way to definitely prove that he was in fact the author, although there are strong arguments that can be made in his favor. He is the only apostle who did not suffer martyrdom. He died peacefully in the year 104 at Ephesus.

PRAYER TO SAINT JOHN

O glorious apostle, Saint John, who for your virginal purity was so beloved by Jesus as to merit to rest your head upon his divine bosom, and to be left, in his place, as a son to his Most Holy Mother, I implore you to set me on fire with a burning love for Jesus and Mary. Obtain for me, I pray, this grace from our Lord, even now, with all my heart set free from earthly affections, I may be made worthy to be united forever here on earth to Jesus as his faithful disciple and to Mary as her devoted child in order to remain united to both of them forever in heaven. Amen.

16. Holy Innocents, Martyrs (December 28)

According to the Gospel of Matthew, King Herod, upon being informed by the Magi of the birth of Jesus, ordered all boys in Bethlehem under the age of two years to be slaughtered, in a vain attempt to snuff out the life of the Lord. However, Mary and Joseph, being warned in a dream that Herod would try something like this, had already fled into Egypt in order to protect the Christ Child. Saint Augustine calls the Holy Innocents the "Flowers of the Martyrs."

KONTAKION OF THE INNOCENTS

When the King was born in Bethlehem, wise men came from the East and brought him gifts. A star had led them on high. As for Herod, he became exceedingly angry, and had the infants harvested like lamenting wheat, and his kingdom came to end.

17. Saint Thomas Becket, Bishop and Martyr (December 29)

Thomas Becket (1118–1170) lived two lives—one a life of flamboyance and great luxury, and the second, a life of simplicity and humble service. Born in 1118, Becket studied law at Merton Priory and at University in London. His father's death left him with little inheritance and so he joined the service of the Archbishop of Canterbury and quickly rose through the ranks. His fortune was made and his reputation was secured when he supported the future King Henry II in a dispute over the throne of England. When Henry assumed the throne, he awarded Becket by making him his Lord Chancellor. In 1161, the position of Archbishop of Canterbury became vacant and Henry, in spite of the objections of Becket, successfully nominated Thomas for the position.

When Becket became the Archbishop of Canterbury, his lifestyle immediately changed, as did his political opinions. He embraced a lifestyle of simplicity and constancy in prayer in all things. In addition he found himself, despite his long friendship with Henry II, at odds with the king over the rights and responsibilities that belonged to the Church and not to the state. Their arguments were intense, at one time so intense that Thomas fled England and sought refuge and protection from the King of France. After Henry and Becket were reconciled, both their friendship and their disagreements continued. At one point, King Henry, particularly frustrated with Becket mumbled "that he wished Becket to be dead." Four of his knights took him at his word and murdered Thomas Becket in his cathedral on December 29. The murder shocked everyone, and King Henry did penance for the act. Thomas Becket was immediately pronounced a martyr and three years later was canonized a saint by Pope Alexander III.

The events that led up to the martyrdom of Thomas Becket can be viewed in the film *Becket* (1964) and read about in T. S. Eliot's famous play, *Murder in the Cathedral*.

PRAYER TO SAINT THOMAS BECKET

Saint Thomas, the Lord gave you the courage to witness to the Gospel of Christ, even to the point of giving your life for it. By your prayers, help me to endure all suffering for love of God and to seek the Lord with all my heart, for God alone is the source of my life. Be mindful of my needs, dear saint, and grant my petition that through your intercession I may be made whole. I ask this through our Lord Jesus Christ, who lives and reigns for ever and ever. Amen.

18. Feast of the Holy Family
(December 30 or Sunday within the Octave of Christmas)

The Holy Family consists of Jesus, the Blessed Mother, and Saint Joseph. Traditionally, the family is portrayed in art with Jesus as an infant or a young boy, reflecting the long-standing belief that Saint Joseph had died before Jesus became an adult. The family is portrayed in perfect union and cooperation, and many of the great saints of the church would speak of this family unit as a symbol of the Church.

A CONSECRATION TO THE HOLY FAMILY

O Jesus, our most loving Redeemer, who came into the world to enlighten us with your teaching and example, did will to pass the greater part of your life in humility and in obedience to Mary and Joseph in the poor home of Nazareth, and in this way sanctifying the family that was to be an example for all Christian families, graciously receive our family as it dedicates and consecrates itself to you this day. Defend us, guard us, and establish among us your holy fear, true peace, and unity in Christian love: in order that by conforming ourselves to the divine pattern of your family, we may be able, all of us without exception, to attain eternal happiness.

Mary, dear Mother of Jesus and our Mother too, by your kindly intercession make our humble offering of this consecration acceptable in the sight of Jesus, and obtain for us his graces and his blessings.

O Saint Joseph, most holy guardian of Jesus and Mary, assist us by your prayers in all our spiritual and temporal necessities, so that we may be encouraged to praise our divine Savior, Jesus, together with Mary and with you, for all eternity. Amen.

19. Saint Sylvester I, Pope (December 31)

Sylvester was a Roman who became pope on January 31, 314. Little is known of his life before he became the pope, and of his reign as pope two events are notable, one is fact and the other is fiction. The event that is factual is that he was pope when the Emperor Constantine issued the Edict of Milan, which provided a period of peace and prosperity, free from persecution, for the Christians of the empire. The event that was fiction is the story that when Sylvester baptized the Emperor Constantine he was freed from leprosy. In grateful thanks, the emperor gave the Church title to vast lands and properties, what is known today as the forgery the donation of Constantine, which was the source of all sorts of problems for the Church and the state in the years that followed. Sylvester died in 335.

PRAYER TO SAINT SYLVESTER I

Holy Saint Sylvester, you witnessed great changes in your lifetime. You well understood the great stress that can accompany big changes, even if those changes are long-hoped-for and welcome, so please pray for me now at this time of great change in my life. Sometimes it seems as if my entire world has been turned upside-down; what I expected has disappeared, and in its place I find situations and events that I never anticipated and for which I feel completely unprepared. Send your spirit to me, to guide me through the uncertainty. Bless my efforts, especially those made in faith. And encourage me with the sure knowledge that all will turn out to be in accord with God's will. In Jesus' name, I pray. Amen.

20. Feast of Mary, Mother of God (January 1)

The most important truth about the Blessed Virgin Mary is that she is the Mother of God. The title "Mother of God" was applied to Mary at the Council of Ephesus in 431 and confirmed at the Council of Chalcedon in 451. This divine motherhood is the source of all Mary's privileges and graces. It is the source of the entire honor that is given to her. Through the centuries, the Church has constantly avowed, as at the third Council of Constantinople, that Jesus Christ was born "of the Holy Spirit and the Virgin Mary, rightly and truly the Mother of God according to his humanity."

Though the title "Mother of God" is not found directly stated in the New Testament, similar terms are used, as when Elizabeth calls Mary the "Mother of my Lord," and as in Luke 1:32 where Mary's future Son is called the "Son of the Most High." Mary's position as the Mother of God was anchored in sacred Tradition as early as the time of Saint Hippolytus (d. 235) who asks of those about to be baptized: "Do you believe in Christ Jesus, the Son of God who was born by the Holy Spirit of the Virgin Mary?"

PRAYER TO THE BLESSED MOTHER OF GOD

Virgin Most Holy, Mother of the Word Incarnate, Mother of God, treasurer of graces, and refuge of us poor sinners; we fly to your motherly affection with lively faith, and we beg of you the grace to always do the will of God. Into your most holy hands, we commit the keeping of our hearts, asking you for health of soul and body, in the certain hope that you, our most loving Mother, will hear our prayer. Amen.

21. Saints Basil the Great and Gregory Nazianzen (January 2)

Contemporaries, both bishops and Doctors of the Church, and amazingly, both Saint Basil (329–379) and Saint Gregory (329–389) were born into a family of saints. Both Basil's mother (Saint Emmelia) and his father (Saint Basil the Elder) were saints as was Gregory's father (Saint Gregory Nazianzen the Elder) and his mother (Saint Nonna). In addition, Gregory's two siblings, Saint Caesarius and Gorgonia are saints as is Basil's younger sister (ten children all together) Saint Macrina the Younger. Basil however is one up on Gregory because his grandmother, Saint Macrina the Elder is also a saint.

In addition to coming from families of saints, Basil and Gregory are well remembered in their own right. Basil is acclaimed as the founder of Eastern monasticism; he was a bishop beyond reproach, known for his orthodoxy, his strength of character, his wisdom and leadership, and his scholarship. He was a giant of a man in a time of great turmoil in the Church. Gregory, a little quieter and the more contemplative of the two, is often surnamed "the Theologian," because of his eloquent defense of orthodoxy, especially the degrees and teachings of the great Council of Nicea in 325. Gregory is also remembered for his great sermons on the Holy Trinity and, along with Saint Basil, a selection of writings by Origen.

Saint Basil died in Caesarea on January 1, shortly after the Emperor Valens died on the battlefield and the Emperor Gratian ascended the throne, effectively ending the spread of the heresy of Arianism, which he fought against his whole life. Saint Gregory died, after retiring to a private and quiet life, on January 25 in Nazianus. He had earlier determined to retire from his see in order to end a controversy, a magnanimous act that convincingly demonstrated his humility and sense of service to the gospel.

PRAYER IN HONOR OF SAINT BASIL

Basil, most honorable, what a noble and divine honeybee you are in the Church of Christ! You armed yourself with divine love, brought down heresies insulting to God, and stored the sweetness of true worship in the faithful's hearts. Now that you have attained the delights of the divine Presence, remember us before the Consubstantial Trinity! Amen.

PRAYER IN HONOR OF SAINT GREGORY

The sweet melody of your theological teachings has overcome the noisy blasts of orators, for God has granted you the power of penetrating spiritual depths, and the gift of brilliant literary talent. Gregory, our Father, intercede with Christ God that he may save our souls. Amen.

22. Saint Elizabeth Ann Seton, Religious (January 4) *(USA)*

The first native-born citizen of the United States to be canonized a saint, Elizabeth Ann Baley (1774–1821) was born into a wealthy family and baptized in the Episcopalian church. At the age of nineteen, she married William Seton and together they raised a family of five children born within a period of eleven years. Because of illness and business failure, life was difficult for the Seton family, and the stress of the events contributed to the untimely death of William while they were traveling in Italy, a trip that had been taken in the hopes that he would recover. Upon her return to the United States, she converted to Catholicism, primarily because of her devotion to the Real Presence of Jesus in the Eucharist, a fact that nourished her devout and spiritual life and because of her devotion to the Blessed Mother. Her conversion, however, was not a conversion that found support among her family and friends, and as a result of her actions, she was estranged from them.

At the request of her parish priest, Elizabeth Ann opened a school for girls in Baltimore, Maryland. This school became the fertile ground necessary for the seed of a religious community to grow. That religious community, first known as the Sisters of Saint Joseph, is known today as the Sisters of Charity of Saint Joseph based in Emmitsburg, Maryland. Elizabeth Ann, now known as Mother Seton, is the founder of this religious community. In addition to being the founder of a religious community, she was also well known as a composer of music (religious hymns were a favorite) and for her spiritual direction. Elizabeth Ann Seton died on January 4, 1821.

PRAYER TO ELIZABETH ANN SETON

Dear Saint Elizabeth, teach me to pray and to see clearly the mind of Christ as you did in your journey to Catholicism. If my choice is the right one, beseech Jesus to bestow his grace on my efforts. If my choice is a wrong one, intercede for me so that my heart may find the better way. Amen.

23. Saint John Neumann, C.Ss.R., Bishop (January 5) *(USA)*

A Redemptorist, the first American bishop to be canonized, John Neumann (1811–1860) was born in Bohemia. From a very early age he determined that he would be a priest but the seminaries in Bohemia were full and very few ordinations were approved. Persisting in his effort, John wrote to the Archbishop in New York City who agreed to ordain him. After ordination, John was assigned to a "parish," which was really most of western New York state. He was soon exhausted and, as well, he desired the support and the nourishment of a religious community. He joined the Redemptorists, becoming the first Redemptorist (1842) to profess religious vows in the United States. However, his life in community was limited. Ten years later, despite his protestations, which were ignored, and despite the protestations of the wealthy families of Philadelphia who did not want an immigrant to be their leader, he was named Bishop of Philadelphia.

Bishop John can best be described as a man who was absolutely dedicated to the poor and the most abandoned. He was fluent in at least six languages and, when Irish immigration started, he also learned Gaelic. He learned the language so well that one Irish woman remarked, "Isn't it grand that we have an Irish bishop." He was also dedicated to the Catholic school system and ensured that the system in Philadelphia would flourish. He is also fondly remembered as the person who initiated the Forty Hours Eucharistic Devotion throughout the United States. Saint John Neumann collapsed in the streets of Philadelphia on his way to the post office to mail a chalice to a poor priest who needed one. He was only forty-eight years old.

PRAYER OF SAINT JOHN NEUMANN

My God, how great Thou art, how wonderful in all your works! Teach me your will that I may begin and end all my actions for your greater glory. Speak to me, O my God, and let me know your will, for I am ready to fulfill everyone of your commands. The difficult, the irksome, I will patiently endure for your love. O my God, I thank you for the love that you have planted in my heart. I will cultivate this precious flower. I will guard it night and day that nothing may injure it. O Lord, water it with the dew of your grace. Amen.

24. Blessed Andre Bessette, Religious (January 6) (North America)

Alfred Bessette, later to be known as Brother Andre, was born on August 9, 1845, near Montreal. The sixth of ten children he was often ill and, as a result, received very little formal education. At twenty-five, he joined the Holy Cross Brothers, who assigned him to menial tasks—his first assignment was as porter (the keeper of the door) at Notre Dame College. He used to joke, "At the end of my novitiate, my superiors showed me the door, and I stayed there for forty years."

In 1904, Brother Andre asked the Archbishop of Montreal if he could have the necessary permission to build a chapel to Saint Joseph on the mountain near the college. The archbishop gave him the necessary permission, and with a few hundred dollars, he built a small wooden shelter fifteen feet by eighteen feet and dedicated it to Saint Joseph. Today that little shelter is the magnificent basilica on the mountain that is a prominent fixture in the landscape of the city of Montreal. It is known as a place of pilgrimage, a place of prayer and devotion, a place of healing of both mind, body, and spirit, but most of all, the place built by the humble lay brother, Brother Andre. He died a peaceful death on January 6, 1937, and was beatified by Pope John Paul II on May 23, 1982.

BROTHER ANDRE'S FAVORITE PRAYER TO SAINT JOSEPH

O Joseph, virgin-father of Jesus, most pure Spouse of the Virgin Mary, pray every day for us to the same Jesus, the Son of God, that we, being defended by the power of his grace and striving dutifully in life, may be crowned by him at the hour of death. Amen.

25. Saint Raymond of Peñyafort, Confessor (January 7)

Saint Raymond of Peñyafort (1175–1275) was a lawyer and a canonist who joined the Dominican's at the age of forty-seven, after already establishing himself as a teacher of renown. He became a great preacher and much sought-after confessor. He was called to Rome by Pope Gregory IX to be his personal confessor and while in Rome he collected and organized Church laws. This collection became an important resource for the Code of Canon Law, which was promulgated in 1917.

Appointed the Archbishop of Tarragona, Spain, he was permitted to decline the appointment because of ill health. Two years after declining, he was elected to succeed Saint Dominic as the master general of the Dominican Order. He served as master general for only two years, at which point he resigned and for the next thirty-five years devoted his life to preaching. He died at the age of one hundred years old.

PRAYER TO SAINT RAYMOND OF PEÑYAFORT

Holy Saint Raymond, the Lord gave you many gifts—of longevity, languages, legal understanding, and administration—and you used your gifts wisely, for God's glorification. Help me to accept the gifts the Lord has bestowed on me, to use them to the fullest of my abilities and not to squander what I have been given. Help me also to realize that the future is not something I will merely inhabit: it is something to create, and in this creative work, my only limitations are my own efforts. Pray for me, then, that I will accomplish the great things that God wants me to do. I ask this through Jesus, our Savior. Amen.

SECTION EIGHT

The Christmas Season

1. Celebrating Christmas

A complaint that is often heard is the expressed perception that "it seems that the Christmas season begins earlier and earlier each year." The perception is based on the common experience of people who can't help but notice that the Christmas displays in the stores appear with the first hint of the end of summer. Certainly it is not uncommon to receive a Christmas catalog in the mail at almost the same time the children are returning to school. Perhaps the season begins earlier and earlier because of the emphasis on the "bottom line" or the "margin of profit," since so many shops and stores count on the Christmas shopping season for a significant part of their business.

From a liturgical perspective, the season of cheer and good will seems to be in contradiction to the emphasis of the season of Advent, which is supposed to be the preparation period for the feast. Most families, if the truth be told, spend the days before Christmas not quietly preparing for the coming of the Lord or waiting for the final coming of the Lord in the end of time, but rather in a frantic shopping and decorating pace. It seems that the liturgical season has succumbed to the secular season of shopping and office parties. Christmas, the time before and the time after the feast, is no longer just a Christian liturgical feast, it has been secularized to the point that it is even celebrated in countries that are officially atheistic. It is a fact that we must acknowledge, albeit reluctantly. But yet, if the spiritual rhythm of the Advent time of preparation, followed by the Christmas time of celebration is entered into, a power may be discovered that will not be lost when the Christmas tree is taken down and the fancy silverware is put away until next year. The pages that follow are one small contribution to this spiritual effort in renewal.

A SHORT HISTORY OF THE CHRISTMAS FEAST

The history of Christmas predates the birth of Jesus. In fact, the history of Christmas can easily be traced back over four thousand years, beginning with the Mesopotamian celebration of the New Year. The Mesopotamians believed in many gods but their chief god, the god Marduk, was expected each year to battle with the monsters of chaos that arrived with the beginning of winter. To assist their god in the struggle, they held a festival for the New Year. This festival, Zagmuk, lasted for twelve days.

In addition to the Mesopotamians, the Persians and the Babylonians celebrated a similar festival, which they named Sacaea. Early Europeans, Scandinavians, and Greeks all had similar festivals.

The Romans celebrated their god Saturn and, as may be expected, it was this celebration that had the most direct influence on the Christian feast of Christmas. The Roman feast began in the middle of December (December 17–21) and ended January 1. The celebrations of the feast included festive meals, visiting friends, and the exchange of gifts call *strenae*, "lucky fruits." The Romans decorated their houses with garlands of laurel and green trees lit with candles. The early Christians of Rome considered it to be an abomination to honor a pagan God in this way and forbid the celebration of the feast, which was quite a problem, especially among the new converts who enjoyed the festival and were reluctant to give it up. Eventually, probably around the year 98 but most certainly by the year 137, the Christians adopted the pagan Saturnalia festival and made it a festival fit for the Son of God in the person of Jesus.

At first the celebration of the birth of Jesus on December 25 (the day the winter solstice occurred according to the Julian calendar) in the Western Church and January 6 in the Eastern Church (the actual date of his birth is not known) was a simple feast. By the fifth century, the feast marked the beginning of the Church year and remained so until the season of Advent took shape after 900. By the twelfth century, it had become the most important religious festival in Europe, and in the fifteenth and sixteenth centuries, many artists of that time painted what are today the most familiar scenes of the Nativity. At the time of the Reformation in the sixteenth century, there was a period where some Christians rejected the traditions and customs of the season, and Christmas was outlawed in England and in parts of the English colonies in America. However, the old customs of feasting and decorating soon reappeared, and Christmas again became a major festival.

The word *Christmas* comes from the English *"Cristes maesse,"* meaning Christ's mass. It might also be observed that the word *Xmas* is sometimes used instead of Christmas. This tradition traces its use to the fact that X is the first letter of the name of Christ in Greek and, as a result, X was frequently used as a holy symbol.

CELEBRATORY NATURE OF CHRISTMAS

If the Advent season is a time of preparation, the season of Christmas is most definitely a time of celebration. Most of the customs and traditions associated with the feast are celebratory in nature, celebrating not only the birth of Jesus but also, in a very real sense, celebrating life. Perhaps it is because of the presence of the Infant Jesus, an infant with the power that all infants seem to embody to bring people to a point of quiet reflection of thankfulness and praise. There are not many people who can look at a small infant and not think of the fragileness of life and the wonder of creation. For many reasons, and possibly because of the atmosphere that surrounds the season, there is a sense of celebration. There is no other time of the year when the landscape is so drastically changed, when lights and garlands and trees, when brightly covered packages and an abundance of good cheer seem to be present everywhere.

Unfortunately, because of the celebratory nature of the feast and because of the expected gatherings of family and friends, Christmas is also a time when many people feel very much alone and unloved. It is, therefore, a time when all people of good will are called to a heightened awareness of the shared humanity that we all possess. This awareness often prompts people to a sense of inclusion instead of the exclusion that is symbolized by "no room in the inn."

TRADITIONAL HYMNS OF CHRISTMAS

There are many hymns associated with Christmas. Some of the hymns such as "Joy to the World," evoke strong spiritual images and still others such as Irving Berlin's "White Christmas" were birthed in a secular environment (the movie *Holiday Inn*) but nevertheless evoke themes of home and family which are most appropriate for the celebration of the season.

Other popular hymns include "Angels We Have Heard on High" from the eighteenth-century French hymn *"Les anges dans nos campagnes,"* "Silent Night, Holy Night" from Franz X. Gruber's (1787–1863) *"Stille Nacht,"* and "What Child Is This," penned by William C. Dix (1827–1898) and sung to the English melody "Greensleeves."

Angels we have heard on high
Sweetly singing o'er the plains,
And the mountains in reply
Echoing their joyous strains
Gloria in excelsis Deo
Gloria in excelsis Deo

Silent Night, Holy Night
All is calm, All is bright,
Round yon Virgin, Mother and Child
Holy Infant, so tender and mild,
Sleep in heavenly peace
Sleep in heavenly peace.

What child is this, who laid to rest
On Mary's lap is sleeping?
Whom angels greet with anthems sweet
While shepherds watch are keeping?
This, this is Christ the King,
Whom shepherds guard and angels sing;
Haste, haste to bring him laud,
The babe, the Son of Mary.

And, finally, there is a hymn composed by Saint Alphonsus Liguori, although it is not as well known as his composition *"Tu scendi dalle stelle,"* it nevertheless captures the spirit of the season. It is entitled, "To the Infant Jesus in the Crib."

Oh, how I love You, Lord of Heaven above!
Too well have you deserved to gain my love;
Sweet Jesus, I would die for your love,
For you did not refuse to die for me.

I leave you, faithless world, farewell, I depart!
This lovely Babe has loved and won my heart.
I love you, loving God from above,
Who came to earth, a child, to gain my love.

You tremble darling child, and yet I see
Your heart is on fire with love for me:
Love makes you a child, my Savior dear,
Love only brought you to suffer here.

Love conquered you, great God, love tied your hands,
A captive here for me, in swaddling bands,
And love, strong love, waits your latest breath,
To make you die for me a cruel death.

2. Some Traditional Practices of Christmas

THE CHRISTMAS TREE

Some claim that Saint Boniface was the first person to decorate a Christmas tree; others claim that Martin Luther was the first to take home a tree and use it as a Christmas decoration. There is evidence, however, that indicates the practice developed out of the medieval religious Paradise play in which a fir tree decorated with apples was used to symbolize the tree of the knowledge of good and evil mentioned in Genesis 2:9. The play told the story of creation, of the sin of Adam and Eve, and of their expulsion from Paradise. It usually ended with the consoling promise of the coming of the Savior and the story of Bethlehem. Obviously, this made the Paradise play a favorite pageant for Advent, usually performed outdoors in front of the church or inside the church. If the pageant was performed inside, lighted candles were placed around the tree, and the play was actually staged within that circle of light. After these plays were no longer performed in church, the Paradise tree found its way into the homes of the faithful, becoming a symbol of the coming of the Savior.

By the fifteenth century, the fir tree decorated with apples was a common tradition. Gradually, small white wafers were added to the apples as decorations for the tree—the wafers symbolizing the Eucharist. The meaning was richly symbolic and deeply rooted in faith and Scripture: the tree which bore the apples, symbolizing the sin of Adam and Eve, also bore the saving fruit of the Eucharist. Later, the wafers were replaced by pieces of white pastry in the form of stars, angels, hearts, flowers, and bells, as well as brown cookies in the form of people, birds, dogs, roosters, and other animals.

By the middle of the seventeenth century, candles, representing Christ as the Light of the World, were placed on the tree. As glass decorations were added to the cookies and the fruit on the tree, our modern Christmas tree came to be. It developed in Germany, gradually was accepted in most other countries, and came to the United States through the German immigrants in Pennsylvania.

THE CRÈCHE

The Christmas tree has been only slowly accepted in Italy, since the predominant symbol in that country was and remains the Nativity scene—the crèche popularized by Saint Francis of Assisi. Francis was devoted to the humanity of Christ who came to us as a baby and died for us amidst suffering. So devoted was he that at the beginning of his ministry, he prayed before a cross in the small country church of San Damiano that was in a state of disrepair. He and his fellow friars restored the church and went around preaching reconciliation of enemies. Francis taught the people to understand how much God loves them by showing them a Nativity scene containing the Christ Child in the manger, with Mary and Joseph nearby, along with the donkey, ox, shepherds, and the three wise men who followed the star to Bethlehem. Francis's devotion to the Christ Child remains an enduring gift that the Italian people treasure.

Another Italian gift to Christmas comes from Saint Alphonsus Liguori, the founder of the Redemptorists, who wrote the Italian equivalent of "Jingle Bells." This song, *"Tu scendi dalle stelle"* ("You Came Down From the Stars"), is the most popular Christmas song in Italy. Men and women dressed like shepherds, using bagpipes, drums, or cymbals for accompaniment, play it on the streets during Advent. The song tells of God's tremendous love for us, so much so that he would send his Son into the cold of night as a tiny baby.

FEAST OF SAINT NICHOLAS

The feast of Saint Nicholas (December 6) celebrates the goodness of the bishop of Ancyra in Syria, who is said to have been devoted to helping children. He became old Saint Nick and Santa Claus in northern European countries and in America. Even into the 1950s—and continuing today—children of German background put out their stockings the night before Saint Nicholas's day, to find them filled with oranges, nuts, and perhaps a bit of candy the next morning. These gifts of goodness are manifestations of God's love to all people.

MIDNIGHT MASS

Midnight Mass has its roots in the early monasteries where people from the countryside gathered in the warmth of the great monastery church to be forgiven, to sing of the newborn Savior, and to participate in the Eucharist. After the religious activities were completed, a great feast took place, lasting well into the morning.

Midnight Mass gathers us together to meet the child Jesus, newly born, and to receive the body and blood of Jesus, newly risen. The readings for the liturgy of Midnight Mass not only proclaim the birth of Christ but also remind us that the grace of God appeared, offering salvation to all people.

CANDY CANES

The simple and familiar red-and-white candy cane is a symbol of the shepherd's crook, the first witnesses of the birth of Jesus. The alternating red-and-white stripes of the candy cane represent the purity (white) and sacrifice (red) of the Lord.

CHRISTMAS HOLLY

The green leaves and the red berries of holly are deeply symbolic. According to an ancient legend, the berries of the holly were once yellow, but were stained permanently by the blood of Jesus, since it was the holly branch that was used for the Crown of Thorns. The ancient Romans used holly as a gesture of good will and friendship during the winter feasts, and so it is quite possible that the tradition of holly at Christmas simply carried over to the Christian celebration of Christmas.

OTHER ETHNIC TRADITIONS

Traditions specific to certain ethnic groups also have an important place in the Christmas season. Hispanics, for example, celebrate *"La Posada,"* the popular retelling of the story of Mary and Joseph searching for a room in the inn. Among people of Slavic origin, the father of the family might break special wafers of bread called *"oplatki"* (a Polish word meaning "thin wafer") on Christmas Eve. The Father distributes these wafers to each person present as a symbol of love and peace. And certainly the Jewish festival of lights, Hanukkah, is an important part of the Christmas atmosphere and celebration.

Prayers Appropriate for Christmas

1. Blessing of the Christmas Tree

Gather around the unlighted Christmas tree. Begin your service by singing "O Christmas Tree" or any favorite carol or hymn.

Reader 1: "Thus says the Lord God: I myself will take a sprig from the lofty top of a cedar; I will set it out. I will break off a tender one from the topmost of its young twigs; I myself will plant it on a high and lofty mountain."

Reader 2: "On the mountain height of Israel I will plant it, in order that it may produce boughs and bear fruit, and become a noble cedar. Under it every kind of bird will live; in the shade of its branches will nest winged creatures of every kind" (Ezek 17:22–23).

PRAYER

Creator God, your own Son is the tender shoot that grew to become a majestic cedar. As birds find safety in giant branches, so we find shelter and comfort in your Son. We thank you for sending us Jesus, our Tree of Life. Amen

BLESSING

Lord God, bless this tree in the name of the Father, and of the Son, and of the Holy Spirit. May it remind us throughout this holy season that Jesus is our Tree of Life.
(Turn on the tree lights.) As we turn on the lights of our tree, we are reminded that Jesus, our Tree of Life, is also the Light of our world. Amen.

2. A Visit to the Sacred Crib of Our Lord Jesus Christ

These words are traditionally prayed at the Basilica of Saint Mary Major in Rome.

I adore you, Incarnate Word, the true Son of God from all eternity, and the true Son of Mary in the fullness of time. As I adore your divine Person and the sacred Humanity united, I feel myself drawn to venerate the poor crib that welcomed you when you were a little child, the crib that was truly the first throne of your love. If there were a way that I could prostrate myself before you with the same simplicity of the shepherds, with the faith of Joseph and the love of Mary, I would choose to do so. If I could bend low to venerate this precious memorial of our salvation with the spirit of mortification, poverty, and humility, which you, the Lord of heaven and earth, chose as a resting place, I would do so! O Lord, you determined in your infancy to be laid in this manger, pour into my heart a drop of that joy which must have been experienced at the sight of your birth. By virtue of your holy birth, I implore you to grant peace and good-will to the entire world. In the name of all humanity, I implore you to give perfect thanks and infinite glory to your Eternal Father, whom, in the unity of the Holy Spirit, lives and reigns one God, world without end. Amen.

3. A Child's Prayer Before the Christmas Crib

Baby on the soft warm hay,
I have a birthday gift for you.
I am wrapping up this whole, long day,
All filled with good things I can do.

I'll help my parents in the house
And try hard to obey.
I'll do a kind deed for my friend,
And I'll be cheerful when I play.

I'll clean my plate at every meal.
I'll put my toys and games away.
I'll go to bed without a fuss
And kneel down silently to pray.

Baby on the soft warm hay,
How do you like my gift today?

4. A Short Christmas Novena

This novena is to be prayed daily, beginning nine days before the feast of Christmas.

I

Eternal Father, I offer to your honor and glory, for my eternal salvation and for the salvation of the whole world, the mystery of the birth of our divine Redeemer. Glory to the Father, and to the Son, and to the Holy Spirit; as it was in the beginning, is now, and ever shall be, world without end. Amen.

II

Eternal Father, I offer to your honor and glory, for my eternal salvation and for the salvation of the whole world, the sufferings of the most holy Virgin and Saint Joseph on that long and weary journey from Nazareth to Bethlehem, and the anguish of their hearts at not finding a place of shelter when the Savior of the world was to be born. Glory to the Father, and to the Son, and to the Holy Spirit; as it was in the beginning, is now, and ever shall be, world without end. Amen.

III

Eternal Father, I offer to your honor and glory, for my eternal salvation and for the salvation of the whole world, the sufferings of Jesus in the manger where he was born, the cold he suffered, the tears he shed, and his tender infant cries. Glory to the Father, and to the Son, and to the Holy Spirit; as it was in the beginning, is now, and ever shall be, world without end. Amen.

IV

Eternal Father, I offer to your honor and glory, for my eternal salvation and for the salvation of the whole world, the pain which the divine child Jesus felt in his tender body, when he submitted to the rite of circumcision. I offer you that Precious Blood which he shed for the salvation of all humanity. Glory to the Father, and to the Son, and to the Holy Spirit; as it was in the beginning, is now, and ever shall be, world without end. Amen.

V

Eternal Father, I offer to your honor and glory, for my eternal salvation and for the salvation of the whole world, the humility, mortification, patience, charity, and all the virtues of the child Jesus. I thank you, I love you, and I bless you infinitely for this ineffable mystery of the Incarnation of the Word of God. Glory to the Father, and to the Son, and to the Holy Spirit; as it was in the beginning, is now, and ever shall be, world without end. Amen.

V. The Word was made flesh.

R. And dwelt among us.

Let us pray. O God, whose only-begotten Son appeared in the substance of our flesh, grant that through Jesus, whom we acknowledge to be like us in all things but sin, we may deserve to be renewed in mind and in spirit. You who live and reign, world without end, forever and ever. Amen.

5. Prayer of Saint Bernard of Clairvaux

Let your goodness Lord, appear to us, that we, made in your image, may conform ourselves to it. In our own strength we cannot imagine your majesty, power, and wonder nor is it fitting for us to even try. But your mercy reaches from the heavens, through the clouds, to the earth below. You have come to us as a small child, but you have brought us the greatest gift, the gift of your eternal love. Caress us with your tiny hands, embrace us with your tiny arms, and pierce our hearts with your soft, sweet cries. Amen.

6. Jesus, Sweetest Child

To be prayed from Christmas to Epiphany.

V. O God, come to my assistance.

R. O Lord, make haste to help me.

V. Glory to the Father, and to the Son, and to the Holy Spirit.

R. As it was in the beginning, is now, and ever shall be, world without end. Amen.

I

Jesus, sweetest child, who came down from the bosom of the Father for our salvation, who was conceived by the Holy Spirit, who did not abhor the Virgin's womb, and who, being the Word made flesh, did take upon yourself the form of a servant, have mercy on us and on the whole world.

II

Jesus, sweetest child, who with your Blessed Mother, visited the home of Elizabeth and Zechariah, who filled your prophet and forerunner, John the Baptist, with your Holy Spirit, and sanctified him in his mother's womb, have mercy on us and on the whole world.

III

Jesus, sweetest child, born in Bethlehem of the Virgin Mary, wrapped in swaddling clothes and laid in the manager, announced by the angels and visited by the shepherds, have mercy on us and on the whole world.

V. Hail Mary, full of grace, the Lord is with you!

R. Blessed are you among women and blessed is the fruit of your womb.

V. Christ is near to us!

R. Come, let us adore him.

IV

Jesus, sweetest child, manifested by the star to the three Magi, worshiped in the arms of your mother, presented with the gifts of gold, frankincense, and myrrh, have mercy on us and on the whole world.

V

Jesus, sweetest child, presented in the Temple by your parents, taken up in Simeon's arms, and proclaimed to Israel by the prophet, Anna, have mercy on us and on the whole world.

VI

Jesus, sweetest child, pursued by the wicked Herod to be killed, carried by your mother and Saint Joseph into Egypt, rescued from the cruel slaughter of the innocents, and glorified and praised by the martyrs blood, have mercy on us, and on the whole world.

V. Hail Mary, full of grace, the Lord is with you!

R. Blessed are you among women and blessed is the fruit of your womb.

V. Christ is near to us!

R. Come, let us adore him.

VII

Jesus, sweetest child, who returned from Egypt to the land of Israel with your parents, suffered many hardships on the way, and entered the city of Nazareth, have mercy on us and on the whole world.

VIII

Jesus, sweetest child, who dwelled in Nazareth with your parents, wearied by poverty and by toil, and increased in wisdom, age, and grace have mercy on us and on the whole world.

IX

Jesus, sweetest child, brought to Jerusalem at the age of twelve, sought by your sorrowing parents, and found with joy after three days in the midst of the teachers of the law, have mercy on us and on the whole world.

V. The Word was made flesh.

R. And dwelled among us.

V. Christ has revealed himself to us.

R. O come, and let us worship.

Let us pray. Almighty and everlasting God, Lord of heaven and earth, who has revealed yourself to little ones, grant that we who venerate with honor the sacred mysteries of your Son, the Child Jesus, may enter into the kingdom of heaven which you have promised to the pure of heart. We ask this through the same Christ, our Lord. Amen.

7. Guided Imagery: The Stable of Bethlehem

A type of prayer that has often proved helpful to people is a prayer form identified as guided imagery. In this prayer form, the use of images, pictures that form in the mind, serves as a platform from which prayer is launched. Guided imagery is a prayer form that is popular with people who are sensate in their perception of the experience of life. As in any type of prayer form, it is meant only to be used as a guide and help.

In the guided images that follow, it may be helpful to recall three essential components of the experience of prayer that are universally helpful: place, time, and freedom.

Place: It is important that you choose a place for meditation and prayer that provides the necessary atmosphere for reflection and that does not cause too many distractions. Whatever place you choose needs to be quiet, comfortable, have the necessary lighting, and have a sense of "welcoming" about it. You need to be able to look forward to your experience of prayer, and you need to feel welcomed and accepted in order to look forward to something.

Time: Choose a time each day when you are most alert and when you are most receptive to ideas, images, and communication. The time that you choose is an essential component. If you are a morning person, for example, you should choose a time that is in the morning. If you are more alert in the afternoon, choose an afternoon time slot. Try to avoid "peak" periods in your daily routine when you are most likely to be disturbed.

Freedom: Freedom is understood as a "stance toward life," permission to be who you are, exactly as you are, and not as you "one day may be." Freedom is also understood as the willingness to be gentle with yourself and to be open to coming to an understanding of who you are as a person.

In guided imagery it is very important to let the images come and go as they are suggested and not to try and force something that is not present. The guided imagery that follows is envisioned for twelve prayer periods. The images invoke traditional Catholic themes and are in two parts. The first prelude, as it is named, provides the suggested image that you are to imagine as an aid to your prayer. The second prelude offers a specific suggestion for intercessory prayer.

MEDITATION I

First Prelude: Enter in spirit the cave of Bethlehem, and behold Mary and Joseph profoundly adoring the divine Child lying in the manger.

Second Prelude: Unite with them in heartfelt adoration and beg them to obtain for you from the divine Infant the grace to grow in faith.

MEDITATION II

First Prelude: Place yourself in spirit on the plain of Bethlehem, and with the shepherds listen to the word of the angel, "I bring you tidings of joy." Filled with joyful hope, enter the stable of Bethlehem with the shepherds.

Second Prelude: Beg the Blessed Virgin and Saint Joseph to assist you in this meditation, in order that the virtue of hope may be increased in your soul.

MEDITATION III

First Prelude: Ask your guardian angel to conduct you to the stable of Bethlehem. The Blessed Virgin and Saint Joseph, with eyes sparkling with love, are gazing on the holy Child and adoring him. Imitate their example.

Second Prelude: Beg our Lord, in this meditation, to inflame your heart with divine love.

MEDITATION IV

First Prelude: Enter in spirit the grotto in which the divine Infant is lying in the manger. Cast a reverential look on the Blessed Virgin and Saint Joseph, and be gladdened by the love and affection that beams from their countenances. Kneel down and with them adore the infant Jesus.

Second Prelude: Beg the grace to understand the tender love of the infant Jesus for all of humanity and to be filled with his love.

MEDITATION V

First Prelude: Imagine yourself in the little town of Bethlehem. See before you the gloomy cave and the manger in which lies the infant Jesus. Enter in spirit and cast a look at the poor simple clothing of Mary and Joseph.

Second Prelude: Resolve, with the assistance of divine grace, to excite in yourself a practical love for holy Poverty.

MEDITATION VI

First Prelude: Kneel with holy reverence at the entrance to the stable of Bethlehem and inhale in the spirit of the heavenly fragrance of Chastity which greets you.

Second Prelude: As the fruit of this meditation, ask for an enthusiastic esteem of the beautiful virtue of purity of heart, and heroic strength to preserve it as every cost.

MEDITATION VII

First Prelude: Go in spirit into the grotto of Bethlehem. Kneel before the manger of the divine Infant and listen to his prayer: "Behold, I come to do the will of God" (Heb 10:9).

Second Prelude: Ask the infant Jesus, his mother Mary, and Saint Joseph to assist you to gain the end of this meditation, which is an efficacious love of cheerful obedience to the will of God.

MEDITATION VIII

First Prelude: Imagine yourself in the stable of Bethlehem and behold Mary and Joseph kneeling in the most humble attitude before the divine Infant.

Second Prelude: As the fruit of this meditation, ask for the grace of a firm resolution to subdue the desire of vainglory and to strive after genuine humility of heart.

MEDITATION IX

First Prelude: Picture the stable at Bethlehem. How wretched its exterior, how uninviting the interior. It is but dimly lighted, the walls are damp, the floor is littered with straw, and the manger, in which you behold the infant Jesus, is uncomfortable.

Second Prelude: Ask the Blessed Virgin in this meditation to obtain for you from her divine Son the love of mortification, together with the courage and the strength to practice it.

MEDITATION X

First Prelude: Imagine yourself in the lonely cave at Bethlehem. Behold Mary and Joseph engaged in silent prayer at the manger in which the infant Jesus is offering himself to the eternal Father as a sacrifice of love for humanity. In the quiet of night, no sound disturbs the holy stillness and recollection of the stable.

Second Prelude: As the fruit of this meditation, determine to strive effectively after the spirit of prayer and recollection. Ask Jesus, Mary, and Joseph to assist you in obtaining the fruit of this meditation.

MEDITATION XI

First Prelude: Behold Mary and Joseph prostrate in adoration before the manger of the infant Jesus. Kneel there with them and gaze intently on the face of the little Redeemer.

Second Prelude: Begin this meditation with the resolution, aided by divine grace, to awaken within you esteem for prayer, together with the efficacious desire of daily advancing in the spirit of prayer.

MEDITATION XII

First Prelude: Enter the holy cave of Bethlehem and imagine the infant Jesus stretching out his hands and saying, "Behold, I come, O Father, to do your will."

Second Prelude: Begin the meditation with the desire of understanding the virtue of the love of the cross and to strive after it with steadfast fervor.

8. Saint Alphonsus Liguori's Visit to the Most Blessed Sacrament

Please refer to page 95 for an explanation and introduction to this traditional prayer form.

OPENING PRAYER

My Lord Jesus Christ, I believe that you are really here in this sacrament. Night and day you remain here, compassionate and loving. You call, you wait for, and you welcome, everyone who comes to you.

Unimportant though I am, I adore you. I thank you for all the wonderful graces you have given me. But I thank you especially for having given me yourself in this sacrament, for having asked your own Mother to mother me, for having called me here to talk to you.

I am here before you today to do three things: to thank you for these precious gifts, to make up for all the disrespect that you receive in this sacrament from those who offend you, to adore you everywhere in the world where you are present in this living bread but are left abandoned and unloved.

My Jesus, I love you with all my heart. I know I have displeased you often in the past—I am sorry. With your help I promise never to do it again. I am only a miserable sinner, but I consecrate myself to you completely. I give you my will, my love, my desires, everything I own. From now on, do what you please with me. All I ask is that you love me, that you keep me faithful to the end of my life. I ask for the grace to do your will exactly as you want it done.

I pray for the souls in purgatory—especially for those who were close to you in this sacrament and close to your mother Mary. I pray for every soul hardened in sin. My Savior, I unite my love to the love of your divine heart, and I offer them both together to your Father. I beg him to accept this offering in your name. Amen.

VISIT TO THE BLESSED SACRAMENT
APPROPRIATE FOR CHRISTMAS

What heavy expense, what dangerous hazards, some people willingly face to travel to the Holy Land! They want to visit the places where Christ was born, where he suffered, and where he died. We need not travel so far nor face such hazards to be near him. The same Savior lives in the tabernacle of our nearby church. Some pilgrims consider it a great privilege to carry away a little dust from the cave where he was born and from the tomb where he was buried. But think of our privilege: not just a remembrance of his life but the reality of his presence!

A holy religious who was burning with love for the Blessed Sacrament wrote this inspiring letter: "Every good thing that I have comes from the Blessed Sacrament. I have offered myself totally to Jesus in the tabernacle. I can see countless graces left unused in this divine sacrament because souls will not come to ask for them. I can see our Lord's devouring desire to nourish souls from here.

"O wonderful Host in which God's power is so clearly revealed! It embodies everything he has done for us. We need not envy heaven's saints. The God they feast on lives with us too—and with even more marvelous proof of his love! Persuade every soul you can to devote itself to the Blessed Sacrament. I speak like this because this divine bread makes my heart expand with love. I try to do everything I can for Jesus in the Blessed Sacrament."

Angels in heaven, you adore our God constantly. Fill my heart with the burning fire of your love. My Jesus, open my eyes so that I can see how astounding is your love for every single human being. The depth of your love should deepen my love. My Lord, I will love you always, and this alone to please you. I believe in you; I trust in you; I love you; I belong to you. Amen.

SPIRITUAL COMMUNION

My Jesus, I believe you are really here in the Blessed Sacrament. I love you more than anything in the world, and I hunger to feed on your flesh. But since I cannot receive communion at this moment, feed my soul at least spiritually. I unite myself to you now as I do when I actually receive you. Never let me be parted from you.

VISIT WITH MARY

Lovable Lady, Saint Bonaventure called you "the mother of orphans." The orphans he speaks of are sinners who have lost God their Father. Here is such an orphan. I have lost my Father, but I still have you as my Mother. You can put me back into his good graces. I ask you for help because I know you will listen. No one ever cries out to you without being heard. No one who prays perseveringly to you is ever lost. Only those souls who fail to seek your help eventually find themselves in hell. So if you want me in heaven, my Mother, make me call on you constantly.

CONCLUDING PRAYER

Most Holy Immaculate Virgin and my Mother Mary, to you who are the Mother of my Lord, the Queen of the world, the Advocate, the Hope, the Refuge of Sinners, I have recourse today—I who am the most miserable of all. I render you my most humble homage, O great Queen, and I thank you for all the graces you have conferred on me until now, particularly for having delivered me from hell, which I have so often deserved. I love you, O most amiable Lady; and for the love which I bear you, I promise to serve you always and to do all in my power to make others also love you. I place in you all my hopes; I confide my salvation to your care. Accept me for your servant and receive me under your mantle, O Mother of Mercy. And since you are so powerful with God, deliver me from all temptations, or rather obtain for me the strength to triumph over them until death. Of you I ask a perfect love for Jesus Christ. From you I hope to die a good death. O my Mother, by the love which you bear to God, I beseech you to help me at all times, but especially at the last moment of my life. Leave me not, I beseech you, until you see me safe in heaven, blessing you and singing your mercies for all eternity. Amen. So I hope. So may it be.

9. Prayer to Mary and Joseph

O Mary and Joseph,
we thank you
for having lived the moments of uncertainty and
anguish
with purity of heart
and with one desire:
to be faithful to the Lord.
God's astounding plan
Made you seek
New directions.
Though frustration was not spared you,
Your faith
Was only strengthened.
Protect us
By your intercession that we may never forget
The presence of our Lord
Who is our joy and our strength.

10. Mary's Firstborn

O Mary,
how great must have been your joy
   in that moment.
Pangs of childbirth,
The anguish of the exodus,
The poverty of the stall
Are only the background of your joy.
You do not have any other treasure but Jesus,
Your firstborn,
And you have no other desire
Than to awaken our trust
In him who is Emmanuel,
God-with-us
Our salvation,
Our joy.
Pray for us
That we may obtain that poverty of spirit
That allows us to find Jesus,
Our only treasure,
Our only love,
And to learn to love with him
All for whom he came
As Savior.
Pray for us
That we may put all our trust in him.
Amen.

11. Prayer to the Infant Jesus
(To be prayed on day 25 of every month.)

O amiable Infant! Although I see you in this cavern, lying on straw poor and despised, yet faith teaches me that you are my God, who came down from heaven for my salvation. I acknowledge you as my Lord and Savior, but I have nothing to offer you. I have no gold of love, because I have loved creatures; I have loved my own desires, but I have not loved you, O amiable infinite one! I have not the incense of prayer, because I have lived in a miserable state of forgetfulness of you. I have no myrrh of mortification, for I have often displeased your infinite goodness so that I would not be deprived of my miserable pleasures. What then shall I offer you? I offer you my heart, filthy and poor at it is, please accept it and change it. You came into the world for this purpose, to wash the hearts of humanity from their sins by your blood, and thus change them from sinners into saints. Therefore, give me this gold, this incense, and this myrrh. Give me the gold of your holy love; give me the incense, the spirit of holy prayer, give me the desire and strength to mortify myself in everything that displeases you. I am resolved to obey you and to love you, but you know my weakness. Give me the grace to be faithful to you! Most holy virgin, you who welcomed the Magi with affection, welcome me also, who has come to visit your Son and to offer myself to him. O my Mother, I have great confidence in your intercession. Recommend me to Jesus. I trust to you my soul and my will; bind it forever to the love of Jesus. Amen.

The Way of Bethlehem

1. Experiencing God Incarnate

The Reverend Robert Aston Coffin, C.Ss.R., writing at Saint Mary's Church in Clapham, London, England, in the month of September 1854, noted that "the time, the manner, the place of the nativity, the cold damp cave, the manger and the straw, the breath of the animals with whom Jesus shared his resting place," all of these details were, for Saint Alphonsus, expressions of that which is great, wonderful, and divine. As such, each detail of the infancy of Jesus suggested a point of meditation and a departure point for prayer.

"If," Father Coffin continues, "with Saint Alphonsus as our guide, we enter the cave of Bethlehem, approach the crib, and gaze on the face of that Divine Child…we would find a boundless, inexhaustible ocean of merit, satisfaction, and grace."

Saint Alphonsus included the "Stations of the Infant Jesus," in the Italian editions of the manuals used for the training of the novices of the Congregation of the Most Holy Redeemer. We have no way of knowing if the stations are by Saint Alphonsus or if they were some devotion that he was familiar with and which he promoted and recommended. Regardless of their origin, the saint viewed the Infant Stations as one way to arrive at a more perfect knowledge and experience of the Incarnate God.

These meditations may be understood as "stations" in the traditional understanding. Each station provided follows the familiar format routinely prayed in the devotion of the Stations of the Cross, with which most readers may have some experience. They are prayed in the same way, although it may be difficult if not impossible to find actual representations of the Infant Stations as easily as one may discover the more traditional Stations of the Cross in most churches. At the very least, the numbers that mark the Stations of the Cross may be used as a reference point so that the Infant Stations may be prayed in a more traditional manner.

2. Stations of the Infant Jesus

V. O God, come to my assistance.

R. Lord, make haste to help me. Glory be to the Father, and to the Son, and to the Holy Spirit. As it was in the beginning, is now and will be forever. Amen.

First Station
The Son of God Becomes an Infant

Consider how the Son of God, the Infinite Majesty, the Creator of the World, who has need of no one, became Incarnate to save lost humanity by his sufferings, and was enclosed for nine months as a little infant in the chaste womb of Mary.

Let us pray: O most amiable infant Jesus, God and man, it was your burning love for me, which prompted you to do all of this. I give you thanks and I beg you, by your Incarnation, to give me the grace to respond to your goodness. O my sweetest Love, I am sorry that I have offended you. I desire to be always faithful in your service. Fill my heart with your love and make me both chaste and holy. O Mary, grant that I may belong entirely to you and to your Son, Jesus.

V. Blessed is the womb of the Virgin Mary, which bore the Son of the eternal Father.

R. And blessed are the breasts that bore you and which gave nourishment to Christ our Lord.

Second Station
Jesus Is Born As an Infant

Consider how Jesus at his birth has not even a wretched cabin, the kind that even poor people have, but is born in a cold cave, and is laid in a manger upon the straw.

Let us pray: O most holy infant Jesus, I thank you for this, and I beg you, by your poor and bitter birth, to grant me the grace of reaping the fruits of your coming on this earth. O my sweetest Love, I am sorry that I have offended you. I desire to be always faithful in your service. Fill my heart with your love and make me both chaste and holy. O Mary, grant that I may belong entirely to you and to your Son, Jesus.

V. Blessed is the womb of the Virgin Mary, which bore the Son of the eternal Father.

R. And blessed are the breasts that bore you and which gave nourishment to Christ our Lord.

Third Station
Jesus Is Fed

Consider how God, Majesty itself, who gives food to humankind and to animals, is born an infant, and who is dependent on Mary for his food. He, through whom even a sparrow is not hungry, is fed with a little milk.

Let us pray: O most lovely Infant, you take milk, to be changed into that flesh which one day is to be torn and bruised for me. I thank you for this goodness and I beg you by this purest milk, to grant me the grace to always act with the pure intention of pleasing you, just as you acted with the sole goal of obtaining my eternal happiness. O my sweetest Love, I am sorry that I have offended you. I desire to be always faithful in your service. Fill my heart with your love and make me both chaste and holy. O Mary, grant that I may belong entirely to you and to your Son, Jesus.

V. Blessed is the womb of the Virgin Mary, which bore the Son of the eternal Father.

R. And blessed are the breasts that bore you and which gave nourishment to Christ our Lord.

Fourth Station
Jesus Is Wrapped in Swaddling Clothes

Consider how the Infinite God, whom the heavens cannot contain, created an Infant for us, to be wrapped by Mary in swaddling clothes and covered with poor rags. By this action the hands and feet of God are tied.

Let us pray: O gentle Infant, you are tied in swathing-bands in order to deliver my soul from the chains of sin and hell. I thank you. Grant, by your holy humility, that every other bond that binds me is cast away so that I may live bound and united to you. O my sweetest Love, I am sorry that I have offended you. I desire to be always faithful in your service. Fill my heart with your love and make me both chaste and holy. O Mary, grant that I may belong entirely to you and to your Son, Jesus.

V. Blessed is the womb of the Virgin Mary, which bore the Son of the eternal Father.

R. And blessed are the breasts that bore you and which gave nourishment to Christ our Lord.

Fifth Station
Jesus Is Circumcised

Consider how the infant Jesus, eight days after his birth, showed himself to be our Savior, by shedding his divine blood for us in the circumcision.

Let us pray: O most merciful infant God, I give you thanks. I beg you, by the pain that you felt, and by the blood with you shed in your circumcision, to grant me the grace and power to pluck out of my heart, and to cast from it, all earthly affections. O my sweetest Love, I am sorry that I have offended you. I desire to be always faithful in your service. Fill my heart with your love and make me both chaste and holy. O Mary, grant that I may belong entirely to you and to your Son, Jesus.

V. Blessed is the womb of the Virgin Mary, which bore the Son of the eternal Father.

R. And blessed are the breasts that bore you and which gave nourishment to Christ our Lord.

Sixth Station
Jesus Is Adored by the Magi

Consider how the infant God is visited and adored by the Magi, who though Gentiles, were enlightened by faith to acknowledge this Man-God as their Savior, and offered to him gifts of gold, frankincense, and myrrh.

Let us pray: Most adorable Redeemer, I, too, have received from you this great gift of faith. I thank you for this gift and I beg you, by the glory of your manifestation, to grant me, like the Magi, to respond in faith and be faithful to your gift of grace. O my sweetest Love, I am sorry that I have offended you. I desire to be always faithful in your service. Fill my heart with your love and make me both chaste and holy. O Mary, grant that I may belong entirely to you and to your Son, Jesus.

V. Blessed is the womb of the Virgin Mary, which bore the Son of the eternal Father.

R. And blessed are the breasts that bore you and which gave nourishment to Christ our Lord.

Seventh Station
Jesus Is Presented in the Temple

Consider how the Virgin Mary, forty days after the birth of the Infant Jesus, carries him in her arms to the temple, and offers him to God for us. Jesus consents to this offering and accepts his role as our Redeemer.

Let us pray: O most loving Infant, for this one purpose you delivered yourself to death, to give me the gift of eternal life. I give you my thanks, and I pray, by this offering of self, that you make me constantly ready to mortify and die to myself for your love. O my sweetest Love, I am sorry that I have offended you. I desire to be always faithful in your service. Fill my heart with your love and make me both chaste and holy. O Mary, grant that I may belong entirely to you and to your Son, Jesus.

V. Blessed is the womb of the Virgin Mary, which bore the Son of the eternal Father.

R. And blessed are the breasts that bore you and which gave nourishment to Christ our Lord.

Eighth Station
Jesus Flees Into Egypt

Consider how Herod, fearing that Jesus would deprive him of his kingdom, plans his death. He orders all the children of Bethlehem to be murdered. The most Blessed Virgin Mary, warned by an angel, takes the Infant into Egypt.

Let us pray: O dearest Infant, what sufferings you endured during this journey of a whole month and even longer, in the depth of winter! How often were you drenched with rain and stiffened with the cold. How many nights did you pass in the open air? I thank you and beg you by your flight to grant me strength to avoid all the dangers of eternal death. O my sweetest Love, I am sorry that I have offended you. I desire to be always faithful in your service. Fill my heart with your love and make me both chaste and holy. O Mary, grant that I may belong entirely to you and to your Son, Jesus.

V. Blessed is the womb of the Virgin Mary, which bore the Son of the eternal Father.

R. And blessed are the breasts that bore you and which gave nourishment to Christ our Lord.

Ninth Station
The Hands of Jesus Are Freed From the Swaddling Clothes

Consider how the infant Jesus, some months after his birth, is still swathed by the Blessed Virgin, although his hands are freed from the swaddling clothes.

Let us pray: Most tender Infant, I imagine to myself that first moment when you joined your little hands, and lifting up your divine eyes to heaven, intercede with the eternal Father on my behalf. I

211

give you thanks and beg you to grant by the merits of your prayer, that I may always be pleasing and acceptable in your sight. O my sweetest Love, I am sorry that I have offended you. I desire to be always faithful in your service. Fill my heart with your love and make me both chaste and holy. O Mary, grant that I may belong entirely to you and to your Son, Jesus.

V. Blessed is the womb of the Virgin Mary, which bore the Son of the eternal Father.

R. And blessed are the breasts that bore you and which gave nourishment to Christ our Lord.

Tenth Station
Jesus Begins to Walk

Consider how the infant Jesus, now a little older, begins to walk, and plans out in his mind the journeys he would make in the surrounding country of Judea to preach the way of salvation. Consider also that at the same time he contemplates the road of Calvary, which he would travel in going to his death for us.

Let us pray: O most loving Infant, I thank you and beg you by your first steps, grant me the grace always to walk in the way in which you pointed out to me. O my sweetest Love, I am sorry that I have offended you. I desire to be always faithful in your service. Fill my heart with your love and make me both chaste and holy. O Mary, grant that I may belong entirely to you and to your Son, Jesus.

V. Blessed is the womb of the Virgin Mary, which bore the Son of the eternal Father.

R. And blessed are the breasts that bore you and which gave nourishment to Christ our Lord.

Eleventh Station
Jesus Sleeps

Consider how the infant Jesus lies in a poor cradle in the little house of his mother Mary, and takes his rest. Often the bare ground is his bed.

Let us pray: O most amiable Infant, even while sleeping your heart watches, and you are loving me and thinking about me. Your heart was consoled with all the good that you would do. I thank you and pray that by your loving slumbers, to give me the grace to live for ever in loving you, who are the most loving good. O my sweetest Love, I am sorry that I have offended you. I desire to be always faithful in your service. Fill my heart with your love and make me both chaste and holy. O Mary, grant that I may belong entirely to you and to your Son, Jesus.

V. Blessed is the womb of the Virgin Mary, which bore the Son of the eternal Father.

R. And blessed are the breasts that bore you and which gave nourishment to Christ our Lord.

Twelfth Station
Jesus Is Considered in the Form of a Fisher

Consider to yourself the infant Jesus represented in the form of a fisher, holding in his hands a rod, to which is attached the hook on which he will catch the hearts of humankind. When we think of his beauty, and when we think of his love for us, and all that he has done to seek us and to attract us to his love, we must consecrate our hearts to his service.

Let us pray: O divine Infant, I give you thanks and pray that the zeal that you have shown in drawing my heart to you, will be the same zeal with which you will keep me to yourself. Grant that I may continue to call on you, that I may become one with you, and that I may never separate myself from you again. O my sweetest Love, I am sorry that I have offended you. I desire to be always faithful in your service. Fill my heart with your love and make me both chaste and holy. O Mary, grant that I may belong entirely to you and to your Son, Jesus.

V. Blessed is the womb of the Virgin Mary, which bore the Son of the eternal Father.

R. And blessed are the breasts that bore you and which gave nourishment to Christ our Lord.

CLOSING PRAYER

I offer and present to you, O most sweet infant Jesus, the stations which I have made to venerate the mysteries of your infancy, and the adoration that I have given you. I pray that you will graciously accept it and reward me with the virtues of childhood—chastity, humility, and simplicity. It is a joy and consolation to me, when I behold you on the altar, surrounded with so many and such lovely flowers. I ardently desire and wish to see my heart adorned with the flowers of virtue so that I may find all my pleasure in you and dwell with you forever. I desire to be united with you in this world and in the next, so that I may dwell in your presence in heaven for all eternity. Amen.

Daily Meditations for Christmas

The emphasis of the Advent meditations is on preparation for the great feast of Christmas. The emphasis of these Christmas meditations is celebration—Christmas and the days that follow up to and including the feast of the Epiphany. Celebration of these days are opportunities to reflect on the significance of the Incarnation. Jesus has become for us the "Word made flesh." (In your planning please note that the feast of the Epiphany is celebrated on January 6, unless it has been assigned in the liturgical calendar for a particular year to the Sunday between January 2 and January 8. This occurs in those places where Epiphany is not celebrated as a holy day of obligation.)

There are many different ways to use the meditations that are provided. A review of the suggested format, first presented in the introduction to the Advent meditations, would include the following steps, often considered essential for fruitful prayer and meditation.

The first step is to choose a particular time each day for your prayer. It is also helpful to choose a particular place that is conducive to reflection and to assume a position that is comfortable. Many people find fifteen or twenty minutes first thing in the morning, before the household awakens, to be very beneficial.

The second step is to quietly read the assigned Scripture for the day. It is not necessary to read the entire Scripture reference, the point is not to "get through everything," but rather to be open to the gentle proddings of the Spirit of God. Some people choose to read just the suggested gospel, others choose just a few lines of text and find it very satisfactory.

The third step is to take some quiet reflection time, just a few moments, and let the Word of God be present to you. After a few moments of quiet, you may then choose to read the meditation that is provided for the day. Again, after reading the meditation, take a few more moments of quiet.

217

The fourth step is to present to God, through prayers of petition, or thanks and praise, the "fruits" of your reflection. For example, the Scripture and the daily meditation might have helped you become aware of your gratefulness for the gift of life or the gift of family. A few simple words of praise and thanksgiving would then be appropriate. Or perhaps you became aware of a relationship that needs mending; a prayer for the other person in the relationship might be appropriate. Whatever comes to you in prayer is considered the "voice of God" or the "gentle prodding of the Holy Spirit."

The fifth step is to conclude your period of prayer and meditation with the slow recitation of a familiar prayer. Some people routinely choose to pray the Lord's Prayer. Still others might choose a prayer from the collections provided in Section Nine of this handbook, "Prayers Appropriate for Christmas."

1. Contemporary Meditations

December 25, Mass at Midnight
Nativity of the Lord (Christmas)
Isa 9:1–6; Ps 96:1–3, 11–13; Lk 2:10–11;
Tim 2:11–14; Lk 2:1–14

Declare his glory among the nations,
his marvelous works among all the peoples.
(Ps 96:3)

One Christmas morning I visited a teenage boy and his mother. They were a single-parent family. The Christmas scene at their home seemed stark and lifeless compared to my own home. I have a large family and our home at Christmas barely holds all of the people, food, gifts, and laughter. But this mother and son I visited were more than content. They had gifts to share with each other, and a love that was deep and abiding. They had no need or want for more. I even felt myself to be a bit of an intruder in such a beautifully calm place.

Jesus, the light of the world and the power of the universe, enters our world as a small child; simple, peaceful, quiet, and calm. There is no need or want for more. The Christmas call is to journey back to the stable, to the inner peace and calm of Mary, Joseph, and Jesus. We embrace Jesus in our midst. He is our light! He is our Power! He is our Peace!

Hopefully you will find time this day to move away from all the gifts, laughter, and filling food that can crowd out the calm of Christmas day. Find the time today to seek out Jesus in the simplicity of his birthing and pray that he will be your light, your peace, your calm, and your gentleness in the year to come. We pray: "Lord, you are born again in my heart this Christmas. Extend your peace to me and through me to my family, friends, community, and world. Be my light always! Amen."

December 26
Saint Stephen, First Martyr
Acts 6:8–10; 7:54–59; Ps 31:3–4, 6–7, 8, 17, 21;
Mt 10:17–22

Let your face shine upon your servant;
save me in your steadfast love.
(Ps 31:16)

Today as we are still flushed with the excitement of Jesus' birth, family togetherness, shared gifts, and food, we are presented with the fairly gruesome picture of Saint Stephen's death. It is true that in the life of Jesus both his birthing and his dying bring us our salvation. It is also true that our own lives are a mixture of births and deaths. Our road to God, like the road walked by Jesus, is often paved with both love and hurt. Today, like Saint Stephen, let us embrace the two great transitions of our lives: our birthing and our dying. We pray: "Lord, it is you who first gave me the breath of life, and it is with you that I will let go of my last breath. Be with me, Lord, daily in my birthings and dyings. Amen!"

December 27

John, Apostle and Evangelist
1 Jn 1:1–4; Ps 97:1–2, 5–6, 11–12; Jn 20:2–8

> *The heavens proclaim his righteousness;*
> *and all peoples behold his glory.*
> *(Ps 97:6)*

Our gospel today proclaims the tradition that John was the first disciple to reach the empty tomb after Mary Magdalene and told them that Jesus' body was gone. The gospel reminds us that John was the disciple that Jesus loved. We know that many years later when Saint John wrote about the birth of Jesus, he said that Jesus was the light that broke into the darkness. The darkness of death, or of sin, or of sickness, or of despair, could no longer imprison Christians if they allow Jesus to be their light. Today we embrace Jesus as our light, we pray: "Lord you are the light, the new dawn, the morning sun! Light my path this day, Lord. Help me to see! Amen."

December 28

The Holy Innocents, Martyrs
1 Jn 1:5—2:2; Ps 124:2–3, 4–5, 7–8; Mt 2:13–18

> *The snare is broken and we have escaped.*
> *Our help is in the name of the LORD.*
> *(Ps 124:7–8)*

Every so often there is a person who is so evil that everyone knows and despises his name. In our own century Adolph Hitler holds such a place in history. In the time of Jesus, this "honor" was held by King

Herod for his massacre of all the boys in his kingdom who were two years old and under. The story of the massacre of the innocent children is retold today in our gospel. This certainly would be a good day to pray for your own children or the children of your extended family. It would also be a time to recommit yourself to protecting your family as Joseph and Mary protected Jesus. We pray: "Lord, in your birth you bring all children under your care. Increase my love and protection for my children. Amen."

December 29

Saint Thomas Becket, Bishop and Martyr
1 Jn 2:3–11; Ps 96:1–2, 2–3, 5–6; Lk 2:22–35

Declare his glory among the nations,
his marvelous works among all the peoples.
(Ps 96:3)

A parent's view of life certainly changes after the birth of their first child. Their hearts embrace the tiny new life that is theirs. Their vision fills with protection and responsibility. The Scriptures today reveal to us how we are to change at the birth of the Lord. Saint John invites us to walk in the light, loving one another, and causing no one to falter. Simeon, in the gospel, asks us to embrace the revealing light of Jesus, which gives meaning to our suffering. We pray: "Lord, open my eyes that I might see and embrace you. Lead me to protect this vision of new life and be responsible to hand this new life to others. Amen!"

December 30

Sixth Day Within the Octave of Christmas
1 Jn 2:12–17; Ps 96:7–8, 8–9, 10; Lk 2:36–40

> *Worship the LORD in holy splendor;*
> *tremble before him, all the earth.*
> *(Ps 96:9)*

Thank God that we are never too old to have fresh visions. Anna, in our gospel, was eighty-four years old. Jesus brought to her a new vision that she had been waiting for and praying for most of her life. Saint John tells us that this new vision will last forever because it is rooted in the Lord and in eternity. Today, we are like Anna and Saint John. We open ourselves to the new vision that is Jesus. We ask Jesus to reveal his way and lead us always in this light-filled path. We pray: "Lord Jesus, like Anna, we await our revelation. Open the doors of our dark ways and let us into the light that lasts through eternity. Amen!"

December 31

The Holy Family of Jesus, Mary, and Joseph
Sir 3:2–6, 12–14 or 1 Sam 1:20–22, 24–28; Ps 128:1–2, 3, 4–5;
Col 3:12–21 or Col 3:12–17 or 1 Jn 3:1–2, 21–24; Lk 2: 41–52

> *Happy is everyone who fears the LORD,*
> *who walks in his ways.*
> *(Ps 128:1)*

The Holy Family is amazingly similar to many of today's families. Mother Teresa said this of the Holy Family: "In Jesus, Mary, and Joseph—the Holy Family of Nazareth—we have a beautiful example for us to imitate. What did they do? Joseph was a humble carpenter in order to support Jesus and Mary, providing their food and clothes—whatever they needed. Mary, the mother, also had a humble task—

that of a housewife with a son and a husband to take care of. As a son growing up, Mary would worry that he would have a normal life, that he would 'feel at home' in the house with her and Joseph. It was a home of tenderness, understanding, and mutual respect abounded."

Jesus, Mary, and Joseph understand well how families struggle today. They identify closely with us. Their prayerful intercession is a powerful source of grace for us who wish to imitate them and to create a 'domestic church' that can lead ever more deeply into the mystery of faith. We pray: "Bless my family, Lord! Bond us closer together in love. Shape us into a happier, healthier, and holier family. Make our family into the image of your Holy Family at Nazareth." Lord, I pray with the psalmist: "O God, do not forsake me, until I proclaim your might to all the generations to come" (Ps 71:18).

January 1
Solemnity of Mary, Mother of God
Num 6:22–27; Ps 67:2–3, 5, 6, 8; Gal 4:4–7; Lk 2:16–21

> *May God be gracious to us and bless us*
> *and made his face to shine upon us.*
> *(Ps 67:1)*

There is the story of a young priest who centered his homily on Mary, the Mother of God. The talk sparked an older woman in the community to tell the priest about her travels to Lourdes, Fátima, Medjugorje, and other places where the faithful believe Mary has appeared. The young priest told the woman that there was in fact only one Madonna. The old woman looked at the priest and said: "How could you have studied for fourteen years and not learned the differences among the Madonnas?"

Every day Catholics over the centuries have cultivated a faith in

Mary that promotes pilgrim shrines, appearances of Mary, statues of Mary that cry or smile, divine power issuing from the water of holy places, holy medals, and scapulars. Miracle after miracle issue forth from these shrines, events, and holy objects. Through the centuries these popular practices have offered a conduit to God for many believers. Mary, the Mother of God, has always been a favorite of this popular style of devotional life. Today almost every Catholic church you enter will have a shrine to Mary where people can pray and light a candle.

Here is how Mary appears through the eye of popular faith: Mary is a restorer of health. Thousands of pilgrims come to the Marian shrines yearly for healing. The number of miraculous cures attributed to Mary would number in the thousands. Mary is an intercessor. She will intercede with God on our behalf. Mary is the mother of mercy. She will always ask God's forgiveness for you and receive it. Let us pray to Mary as this New Year begins: "Mary, we ask you to be our perpetual help. Never let us down! Lead us, protect us, and pray to your Son for us in this New Year. Amen."

January 2

Saints Basil the Great and Gregory Nazianzen,
Bishops and Doctors of the Church
1 Jn 2:22–28; Ps 98:1, 2–3, 3–4; Jn 1:19–28

> *All the ends of the earth have seen*
> *the victory of our God.*
> *(Ps 98:3)*

Sometimes in the midst of a quarrel one spouse will yell out to the other: "Don't you ever listen to what I am saying?" Many times we demand of our children: "Did you hear what I said?" In today's Scripture John emphasizes the importance of listening—not just listening with the ears, but listening with the heart. What we have heard from the beginning must remain within our hearts. John the Baptist gave testimony to the Jews that Jesus, the Messiah, was coming. But their ears and, more important, their hearts would not receive this message. Today we listen to the Scriptures and allow the message to sink deeply into our hearts. We pray: "Lord Jesus, you have the words of life. Speak those words to me today that I might live. Amen!"

January 3
1 Jn 2:29–3: 6; Ps 98:1, 3–4, 5–6; Jn 1:29–34

He has remembered his steadfast love and faithfulness.
(Ps 98:3)

Many times when parents look at their teenage sons and daughters it is difficult for them to believe that these large, gangly, boisterous people were once small quiet children. When we think about the birth of Jesus as a small baby, it is also difficult to believe that this child stood with God, was equal to God, and came from God. Our Scripture today reminds us of things that might be difficult to believe. The gospel tells the story of Jesus leaping from the throne of God to earth and John announcing Jesus' anointing. We pray: "Jesus, deepen my belief this day in your power as God. Anoint me and send me forth to love. Amen!"

January 4
Saint Elizabeth Ann Seton, Religious
1 Jn 3:7–10; Ps 98:1, 7–8, 9; Jn 1:35–42

Let the floods clap their hands;
let the hills sing together for joy.
(Ps 98:8)

The adage that "actions speak louder than words" certainly applies to our Scripture today. John reminds us that love of God is centered in our love of our brothers and sisters. As a young man, Jesus called Peter and John, his first disciples to follow him. Peter and John didn't quite know where Jesus would take them, but they believed in Jesus. Today Jesus calls to us to follow him. Unlike Peter and John, we know that this following of Jesus will lead to a commitment. This pledge is to act like Jesus in how we love and honor one another. We pray: "Lord Jesus, open my heart to hear your call. Today lead me to love deeply those whose paths I cross. Amen!"

January 5
Saint John Neumann, C.Ss.R., Bishop
1 Jn 3:11–21; Ps 100:1–2, 3, 4, 5; Jn 1:43–51

> *Know that the LORD is God.*
> *It is he that made us, and we are his.*
> *(Ps 100:3)*

Each of us has a turning point in our adult lives. It could be the moment you fell madly in love and knew that you could not live without this other person in your life. It could be the first time that someone whom you loved very deeply died and you awakened to how precious life is. Today's Scripture recalls for us the familiar story surrounding the call of Philip and Nathanael. It was a turning point, a moment that changed their lives. Let us ask God to change our lives on this day. Bring us to a turning point. We pray: "Lord, you are the center of my life. I turn to you again today. Fill me with hope and promise. Amen!"

January 6

Blessed Andre Bessette, Religious
**1 Jn 5:5–13; Ps 147:12–13, 14–15, 19–20; Mk 1:7–11
or Lk 3:23–28 or 3:23, 31–34, 36, 38**

> *He grants peace within your borders;*
> *he fills you with the finest of wheat.*
> *(Ps 147:14)*

Bumper stickers that proclaim "My son is an honor roll student" or "My daughter gets straight A's" testify to the sense of pride that the parents feel. John the Baptist and the first Christians were equally proud to testify about Jesus. Our Scripture today presents the image that those who are attached to Jesus are a people who are both proud of Jesus and testify to the greatness of Jesus. Today let us reclaim our sense of being a son or daughter of Jesus. Let us testify in our actions and in our prayers that Jesus is the Lord! We pray: "Lord, let me witness and testify that you are my Messiah, my Lord. Let your life abound within me. Amen!"

Epiphany of the Lord

**Isa 60:1–6; Ps 72:1–2, 7–8, 10–11, 12–13;
Eph 3:2–3,5–6; Mt 2:1–12**

> *In his days may righteousness flourish*
> *and peace abound, until the moon is no more.*
> *(Ps 72:7)*

Since the time of the catacombs paintings of the three wise men coming to pay homage to Jesus have been one of the favorite ways of depicting Jesus' manifestation to the whole world. Even the furthest pagan nation is drawn to the brightness of the Lord, which shines in Jerusalem. The question for us today is: "How will the light of Christ shine through me so that all people will see the brightness of Jesus?"

As a people of faith, we are asked to renew ourselves, to change the way we live, and to begin anew. The beginning point of this conversion is the sacrament of penance and reconciliation. This forgiveness will both comfort us and transform us. We will make fresh our relationship with God. We are then to strengthen our family unity by letting go of old grudges and allowing others also to begin fresh. Once reconciled individually and in the family we can then move out into wider circles. Our family can be a small church offering the power of love, forgiveness, and change to social situations and institutions that cause violence, poverty, injustice, and discrimination. Let us truly celebrate the Epiphany of the Lord by making a new beginning. We pray: "Lord, let your light first shine within me. May it comfort and transform me so that I can offer my gifts of love and light to the world. Amen!"

2. Traditional Meditations of Saint Alphonsus

The method of meditation, as proposed by Saint Alphonsus, consists in three parts: *preparation, consideration,* and *conclusion.* In the *preparation* phase, we are to remind ourselves of the presence of God and pray a prayer of humility and a prayer of enlightenment. We conclude the preparation segment of our meditation with a Hail Mary to the Blessed Mother and a Glory to the Father in honor of our guardian angel. In the *consideration* phase, we read the meditation and think about the Passion of Jesus Christ. Saint Alphonsus reminds us that it is important that in the meditation we use our time to produce "affections," prayers of humility, love, sorrow for sin, resignation to the will of God and in making our prayers and petitions known to God. Finally, the *conclusion* phase is made by praying, "I thank you God for the enlightenment that you have given me, I promise to continue to walk with you in love, and I beg from you the grace to fulfill all that I have promised and hoped for." The saint also strongly recommends concluding the meditation with a prayer for the Poor Souls in Purgatory, which can be found on page 89 of this book.

Each of these Christmas meditations are very revealing of the emotional and romantic temperament of Saint Alphonsus. At first the reader might be slightly "put off" by this form of expression, but understood and appreciated within the context of his time, they can, be very helpful for prayer and reflection. Each of the meditations are abridged and edited for today's reader. A meditation is provided for each day of the season, from December 25 to the feast of the Epiphany. (Please note that the feast of the Epiphany is celebrated on January 6, unless it has been assigned in the liturgical calendar for a particular year to the Sunday between January 2 and January 8. This occurs in those places where Epiphany is not celebrated as a holy day of obligation.)

December 25

The birth of Jesus.

Consider that the birth of Jesus Christ caused universal joy in the whole world. Jesus was the Redeemer who had been desired and awaited for so many years. He was called the desire of the nations and the desire of the eternal hills. Today we behold him, born in a little cave! Let us consider that this day the angel also announces to us the same great joy announced to the shepherds. "Behold, I bring you good tidings of great joy, for a savior has been born."

What great rejoicing there is in a country when the firstborn son of a king is born. But surely there should be even greater rejoicing when we see the Son of God born! We were lost and he came to save us. He is the shepherd who has come to save his sheep from death. He is the Lamb of God who has come to sacrifice himself, to become our deliverer, our life, or light, and even our food in the most Holy Sacrament.

Saint Maximus says that for this reason, among many others, Jesus chose to be laid in the manger where the animals are fed, to make us understand that he has been human and also our food. "In the manger, where the food of animals is placed, he allowed himself to be laid, demonstrating that his own body would be the eternal food of humankind." Besides this, he is born every day in the sacrament of the altar; the altar is the crib, and we go to the altar to be fed and nourished. Some might desire to hold the infant Jesus in their arms as the prophet Simeon did, but faith teaches us that when we receive holy Communion, we, too, hold the same Jesus who was in the manger in Bethlehem, not in our arms, but in our hearts.

My beloved Jesus, if I do not love you, who are my Lord and my God, whom shall I love?

December 26
Jesus is born an infant.

Consider the first sign which the angel gave to the shepherds as they discovered the newborn Messiah was that they would find him as an infant. The littleness of infants causes us to respond in love but consider that the infant Jesus, who is also the incomprehensible God, has made himself an infant for our sake. Adam came into the world as a fully developed man, the eternal Word chose to appear to us as an infant, so that he might attract our hearts to himself with great force. He did not come into the world for any other reason other than to be loved.

How is it possible that any person can reflect with faith about God who became a little child and not love him, as did Saint Francis of Assisi who said, "Let us love the child of Bethlehem, let us love the child of Bethlehem." He is an infant, he does not speak, he only cries, but these cries are cries of love which invite us to love him, cries that demand our hearts.

My beloved Jesus, my dearest Infant, enchain me with your love. I love you, and will always love you. Permit me never to be separated from you.

December 27

Jesus in swaddling clothes.

Consider the Blessed Mother, having given birth to her Son, now takes him with reverence in her arms, adoring him as God, and then wrapping him in swaddling clothes. Behold the infant Jesus who obediently offers his little hands and feet and allows himself to be swaddled. Consider that every time the holy Infant allowed himself to be swathed he thought of the cords with which he one day would be bound and led captive from the Garden of Gethsamane. Also consider the cords which secured him to the column on which he was whipped, and the nails which would secure him to his cross. All of this he permitted in order to deliver our souls from the chains of hell. Bound in these swaddling clothes, Jesus turns to us and invites us to unite ourselves with him with the holy bonds of love.

My beloved Jesus, you have imprisoned yourself in swaddling clothes because of your love for me. I will become a prisoner of your infinite love. Bind me tight so that I may never be able to disengage myself from your love.

December 28

Jesus is nourished at his mother's breast.

Consider that Jesus, as soon as he was swathed, looked for and took milk from the breast of Mary. What a spectacle it must have been to those in Paradise to witness the divine Word, who had become an infant, sucking milk from a virgin who was his own creature! Sister Paula, the Camaldolese, in contemplating a little image of Jesus taking milk, felt herself immediately inflamed with a tender love for

God. O my Jesus, permit me to join my voice with the voice of the women in the gospel who proclaimed, "Blessed is the womb that bore you and the breasts that fed you!"

My beloved Jesus, you are the bread of angels. Grant me a tender devotion to your holy infancy so that I may forget everything else and think of nothing but you.

December 29

Jesus lies on the straw.

Consider that the Mother of Jesus has neither wool nor down to make a bed for the tender infant. What does she do? She gathers together a small handful of straw into the manger. How hard and how painful is this bed for an infant that has just been born. The limbs of a baby are so delicate and especially the limbs of Jesus, which were formed by the Holy Spirit with a special delicacy. Straw is a bed fit only for beasts and yet the Son of God had no other bed on which to lie than a bed of miserable straw. Saint Francis of Assisi, while sitting at table one day, reflected on this fact and immediately rose from his place at table, threw himself on the ground, and finished his meal. "What," he said, "my Lord was laid on straw and I continue to sit?"

My beloved Jesus, I do not desire to leave you alone to cry and to suffer. Your tears both afflict and console me. They afflict me because you are so innocent, but they console me because they assure me of the gift of salvation. I, too, will weep because it is my sins that are the cause of your sufferings.

December 30

Jesus sleeps.

Consider that the manger served as Jesus' cradle, straw was his bed, and straw his pillow, so that he was constantly interrupted in his sleep by the hardness and roughness of this little bed. Notwithstanding all of this, the sweet babe, from time to time, slept despite his sufferings. But the sleep of Jesus differed from other children. The slumbers of other children are useful for the preservation of life, but not for the operations of the soul, because the soul, being buried in sleep along with the senses, cannot work, but such was not the sleep of Jesus Christ. Let us ask him, by the merit of his blessed slumbers, to deliver us from the deadly slumber of sinners who unhappily sleep in the death of sin, forgetful of God and of his love. Instead we ask for the sleep of the holy spouse, when the soul forgets all earthly things, to attend only to God and to the things that concern the glory of God.

My beloved and holy Infant, in humans sleep is the emblem of death; but in you, it is the sign of eternal life, because while you are sleeping you merit for me eternal salvation. Make me always love you in this life so that I may breathe forth my soul in your arms, united to you, sleeping with you forever without fear of losing you again.

December 31

Jesus weeps.

Consider the tears of the infant Jesus. The tears of newborn infants are often tears of pain. Jesus did not weep because of pain, but rather because of compassion and love. "They weep because of suffering, Christ because of compassion," says Saint Bernard. Tears are a great sign of love and behold how our God loves us, since for the love of humanity we see Jesus made flesh, become an infant, and shed tears. "These tears," teaches Saint Ambrose, "washed away our sins," because by his cries and tears he implored mercy for us who were condemned to eternal death. Oh, how eloquently did the tears of this divine little one plead in our behalf. How precious were his tears to God. It was then that the Father caused the angels to proclaim that he had made peace with humanity and received them again into his favor. And on earth peace to all people of good will.

My beloved infant Jesus, while you were weeping in the stable at Bethlehem, you were thinking of me. Eternal Father, I offer you the tears of the infant Jesus; for the sake of his tears, please forgive me.

January 1

The name of Jesus is powerful.

Consider that the name of Jesus is a divine name, announced to Mary by Saint Gabriel. For this reason, Jesus is a named identified above all other names. This great name, says Saint Bernard, can be understood as light, food, and medicine, for the name of Jesus is light to the mind, food for the heart, and medicine to the soul. It is light to the mind for by this name the world was converted from the darkness of sin to the light of faith. It is a food that nourishes our hearts because this name reminds us of what Jesus had done for us. Finally, it is medicine to the soul because it makes the soul strong against the temptation of the enemy. Who was ever lost, who was ever tempted, when they called upon the powerful name of Jesus?

My beloved Jesus, I always call upon you my Jesus, and by the power of your name I now hope for all things. In your name I shall discover all that is good.

January 2

The name of Jesus is holy.

Consider that the name of Jesus is a name of gladness, a name of hope, and a name of love. A name of gladness because if the memory of past sins afflicts us, this name comforts us, reminding us that the Son of God became human for this purpose, to make himself our Redeemer. The name of Jesus is a name of hope because the person that prays to the eternal Father in the name of Jesus may hope for every grace. The name of Jesus is a name of love because it is a sign that represents to us how much God has done for our love. The name of Jesus helps us to remember all the sufferings that he endured for us in his life and in his death. As a devout writer says of the holy name, "My Jesus, how much has it cost you to be Jesus—that is to say, my Redeemer!"

My beloved Jesus, write your name on my poor heart and on my tongue in order that when I am tempted to sin, I may resist all sin by invoking your holy name. If I am tempted to despair, your name will help me to trust. If I feel myself becoming tepid in my love for you, your name will inflame my heart. Help me always to call upon your most holy name.

January 3

The solitude of Jesus in the stable.

Consider that Jesus chose the stable of Bethlehem for his hermitage and oratory. Consider that he chose to be born out of the city in order to recommend to us the love of solitude and of silence. There in the stable we can see the poverty of this wandering little hermit, who remains in that cold cave, without fire, with a manger for a crib, and a little straw for a bed. When we hear his cries and behold the tears of this innocent child, and consider that he is our God, how is it possible to think of anything but loving him? Oh, what a sweet hermitage for a soul that has faith in the stable of Bethlehem. Let us also imitate Mary and Joseph who, burning with love, contemplate the great Son of God clothed in flesh.

My beloved Jesus and my dearest Savior, I desire to unite myself to you and to keep you company. Do not reject me. I do not deserve to be in your presence, but I feel that you have invited me through your sweet voice, speaking to my heart. I will come to you, my beloved Infant.

January 4

Occupations of the infant Jesus in the stable.

Consider that there are two principal occupations for a person who is in solitude—to pray and to do penance. Behold the infant Jesus in the little grotto of Bethlehem giving us example by constantly making acts of adoration, of love, and of prayer. How beautiful, perfect, and dear to God were the acts of love and adoration that the Incarnate Word made to his Father. How beautiful, perfect, and dear to God were the prayers of the infant Jesus. Every moment he prayed to his Father his prayers were for us and for each one of us in particular. All that we have received from the Father Jesus has obtained for us by his prayers.

My beloved Jesus, how much do I owe you? If you had not prayed for me, in what state of ruin would I now find myself? I thank you, Jesus, your prayers have obtained for me the pardon of my sins and I hope that your prayers will also obtain for me perseverance until death.

January 5

Poverty of the infant Jesus.

Consider that Jesus, the Son of the Lord of heaven and earth, lies in a cold grotto without a cradle and nothing but straw for his bed and miserable rags to cover him. The angels stand around him and sing his praises, but they do not relieve his poverty. My dear Redeemer, the poorer you are, the more lovable you become to our eyes, because you have embraced so great a poverty to make us love you even more. If you had been born in a castle, if you had a cradle of gold, if you had been attended to by the great princes of the earth, you would have acquired more respect from humankind but less love. But in this stable where you sleep, where miserable rags cover you, where straw is your bed, and where the manger is your only cradle, you attract our souls to love you. You have made yourself poor in order to become even more dear to us.

The poverty of Jesus was for each of us a great source of riches because his example urges us to seek the riches of heaven and to despise those of the earth. My Jesus, your poverty has induced so many saints to leave all—riches, honors, kingdoms—in order to become poor with you.

My beloved Redeemer, detach me from all affection to earthly goods, so that I may be made worthy to acquire your holy love and possess you, who art the infinite good.

Epiphany of the Lord

Adoration of the Magi.

Consider that Jesus is born in a stable, the angels of heaven acknowledge him, but humanity abandons him on earth. Only a few shepherds come and pay him homage. But our Redeemer desired to communicate to all people the grace of his redemption so therefore the eternal Father sends a star to enlighten the holy Magi, in order that they may come and acknowledge their Redeemer. This was the first grace bestowed upon us, our vocation to the faith, which was succeeded by our vocation to grace, of which all people had been deprived.

The wise men, without delay, set off on their journey. The star accompanies them as far as the cave where the holy Infant lies. On their arrival they enter, and what do they find? They find a poor maiden and a poor Infant wrapped in poor swaddling clothes. But upon entering the little shed these holy pilgrims feel a joy that they had never felt before, they feel their hearts chained to the dear little Infant that they see. The straw, the poverty, the cries of the little Savior—what darts of love! The Infant looks upon them with a joyful face. The holy kings then look at Mary, who does not speak, but with her blessed face that breathes the sweetness of paradise she welcomes them. They also, out of reverence, adore Jesus in silence and acknowledge him as their God, kissing his feet, and offering him their gifts of gold, frankincense, and myrrh. Let us also with the holy Magi adore our little King Jesus, and let us offer him all our hearts.

O amiable Infant, I see you in this cave lying on straw, poor and despised, yet faith teaches me that you are God, who came down from heaven for my salvation. I acknowledge you as my Lord and as my Savior. But I have nothing to offer you, I have no gold of love, I have not the incense of prayer, and I have no myrrh of mortification. What, then, shall I offer you? I offer you my heart, filthy and poor as it is. Please accept the gift of my heart and change it for your honor and your glory. Amen.

Family Meal Prayers for the Holiday Season

There is nothing quite like the time between the end of November and the first few days of January. Usually referred to simply as "the holidays," if they didn't exist, surely someone would have to invent them. For what other reason would family and friends gather to spend time together, to bring one another up to date, or to observe the development of relationships—both new and old?

While the holidays mean many things to many different people, there is usually one tradition that remains constant from family to family, namely, the holiday dinner. For many, the evening meal is the anchor of the holiday celebration. It's the one time during the festivities that it's possible to get everyone away from the television, out of the backyard, unhooked from the headphones, to be present to one another in one place—at least for a fleeting moment. Right before the family starts filling their plates, there is that sometimes awkward moment when a prayer seems in order. Everyone turns to Mom, Dad, Grandma, Grandpa, or someone with a reputation for "holiness," and expects him or her to lead the prayer.

It is for that moment when all eyes are on you that these prayers are intended. Instead of fumbling for words or trying to recall the one version of grace that everyone knows, you can turn to the appropriate day and lead the prayer. Each prayer touches on the basic themes of the celebration for which it was written and requires no preparation on your family's part or prompting on yours, just a simple response of "Amen" at the prayer's end.

Mealtime prayers are provided for the following family gatherings: Thanksgiving Day, First Week of Advent, Second Week of Advent, Third Week of Advent, Fourth Week of Advent, Solemnity of the Immaculate Conception (December 8), Feast of Our Lady of Guadalupe (December 12), Solemnity of the Birth of Our Lord (Christmas), Feast of the Holy Family, New Year's Eve, and New Year's Day.

You will notice that religious observances have been mixed with traditional civic holidays. For example, while Thanksgiving is not a holy day in our religious tradition, January 1 is both New Year's Day and the Solemnity of Mary, Mother of God. Thus, any family gathering during the holiday period, whether officially designated as a holy day or not, can be understood and celebrated as holy in the broadest possible sense.

You may have hoped that this list would include other holidays particular to your own family tradition. Don't lose hope. A generic prayer suitable for any occasion has also been included. In this way, you will be prepared for all gatherings, no matter what their focus.

I hope you will enjoy these prayers, even as I have enjoyed compiling them for you. I hope as well to join in spirit with you as you pray them with the people you love. God bless!

1. Thanksgiving Day

Today is a day of turkey and football, or so it seems. In some families, dinner has to be served during halftime or not at all. In other families, the television is turned off, the family gathers around the table, and everyone has to deal with the impatience of the football fans who want to get this "family stuff" over with and back to the real action!

In the midst of this family drama, ask everyone to take a moment to be silent, to try and quiet their thoughts, to forget about football, and to think about the blessings and the abundance that surrounds them. This prayer might serve you well as you help your family celebrate.

O bountiful God,
You have blessed us in ways that
we cannot even begin to number.
We are aware that we take so much for granted.
We assume the abundance before us
will always be ours.

Be with us, members of your family,
    faithful followers of your Word.
Help us to become aware of your gifts
    and not to take even the smallest among them for granted.
Help us to develop a thankful heart
    and a grateful spirit.

Bless the food that we share today.
Bless our family, our friends,
    those who are near and dear to us.
Finally, loving God, remember those who go without:
    the poor, the abandoned, the lonely and forgotten.
We pray in the name of Jesus, our Lord.
R. Amen.

2. First Week of Advent

For many of us, Advent simply fills in the space between Thanksgiving and Christmas. As the Church counts down the time before the celebration of the birth of Jesus, we might find ourselves counting the shopping days left until Christmas.

If you want to join with the Church in this season of preparation, try to pray the following prayer with your family at least once during the First Week of Advent. In this way, you can counteract the commercialism of the season and enter more fully into the spiritual meaning of the time that we celebrate.

O holy Abba God, we are an expectant people, always rushing to accomplish things, only to experience time slipping through our fingers.

We expect things to improve, hoping that somehow we will not always put you, and our relationship with you, on the back burner of our lives.

For this reason, we pause for a moment in prayer. Be with us during this season of Advent. Help us to come to an appreciation of "holy waiting."

As once your people long ago waited for their Savior to be born, help us enter into the spirit of celebrating the growing awareness of your Word in our lives.

Let the power of your Word not be buried or forgotten because of the press of our other obligations.

The food that we share, the relationships that we celebrate, are all signs of your love. Help us appreciate them and enjoy your presence in each of the people, the events, and the experiences that make up our lives.

We pray in the name of Jesus, the Savior.

R. Amen.

3. Second Week of Advent

Whether or not you succeeded in gathering the family together to pray during the past week, there's still a lot of Advent left. You can still enter into the spirit of the season by carving out some sacred space and time in your life and in the lives of those you love. This prayer might make it a little easier for all concerned.

O holy, patient, and loving God,
In this season of grace-filled longing,
we await the coming of your Son and our Savior.
It is difficult for us to remember
    that this is a holy time.
There are so many distractions:
    commitments seem to pile up,
    and expectations are high.

In the midst of our busy world, our busy lives,
    we need your help to remind us
    of what is important and necessary.
While many of those things that we do not need
    will come to us in packages gleaming and bright,
    the one gift that will last comes from you alone,
    gracious God, as we grow in our awareness of your love.
Bless us, our family and friends,
    and the food and the company that we share.
Increase in us a growing urgency
    to celebrate the birth of your Son,
    in whose name we pray.
R. Amen.

4. Third Week of Advent

If you haven't yet succeeded in slowing down, if you find yourself succumbing to the Christmas rush without even thinking about Advent and the spiritual significance of the season, or if you're the type that panics—this is it! With Christmas fast approaching, you're running out of quality Advent time.

Up to this point, you might have been gentle with the family and, under most circumstances, I would congratulate you. Now, however, I counsel a little pushiness. Gather them around the table and pray this Advent prayer.

O almighty God,
Gracious provider and giver of life,
We anxiously await the celebration of your birth.
Like the people of long ago,
our ancestors in faith,
    we, too, are in need of light,
    in need of direction,

in need of your Word, to show us the way.
Our busy lives and the consumerism that surrounds us
    make it difficult to recognize your kingdom
    and to hear your voice.
There are so many other ways,
    other voices that compete for our attention.
Help us, Lord, to focus on you.
Bless our family,
the food we share,
the thoughts,
concerns,
hopes,
and dreams of everyone gathered here.
We pray that you hear our prayer in the name of Jesus.
R. Amen.

5. Fourth Week of Advent

As the family gathers this one last time before the final holiday rush,
suppress any last-minute shopper's anxiety you might be having and
see if you can hear and feel the expectant silence of the creation that
surrounds you.

O creator God,
Our world is pregnant with the anticipation
    of the birth of your Son.
We are bursting in our preparedness,
    for the feast of Christmas will soon be here.
Everything seems to be in order:
    the plans are agreed to,
    the tree is decorated,
    most of the gifts are wrapped,
    and we think we are ready.

However, Lord, as we pause to offer this prayer,
    we realize that some things have been rushed,
    and, in the process,
    some important things have been forgotten.
In this brief moment of quiet,
help us to be at least thankful.
Help us to appreciate the Word
    that comes to dwell with us.
Help us to hope in the promise of his way,
    truth, and life.
Help us to join with the angels who sing your praise.
Bless our food.
Bless your people.
Grant us the lasting peace of this great season of joy.
We pray in the name of our long-expected Lord.
R. Amen.

6. Solemnity of the Immaculate Conception (December 8)

The Solemnity of the Immaculate Conception is a holy day of obligation in the United States. While today's feast celebrates the fact that our Blessed Mother was conceived without original sin, it is often misunderstood to be a commemoration of the virgin birth of Jesus. Perhaps it is because this feast occurs so close to Christmas, or because it has never been properly explained. In any case, much confusion remains.

This simple prayer will serve not only as grace for your evening meal but also to summarize the central point of the dogma of the Immaculate Conception. Maybe, as a result of praying this prayer, members of your family might come to a new understanding of this feast, or at least some discussion might follow.

O holy and loving Creator God,

From the beginning of time

You have loved and called your people into life.

You have blessed each of us

>with an abundance of grace

>and with the presence of your life-giving Spirit.

In a special way,

>you loved and called our Blessed Mother into life,

>free from the stain of original sin.

From the moment of her conception,

>she was completely open to the power of your Word,

>willing to follow your will unreservedly.

May we share in her willingness to believe,

>to risk,

>and to hope in the power of your presence.

Bless our family gathered here,

>as once you blessed the Holy Family

>as they, too, gathered together

>to be nourished and fed with the food that you provide.

We pray through the intercession of our Blessed Mother,

and in the name of Jesus, the Lord.

R. Amen.

7. Feast of Our Lady of Guadalupe (December 12)

The feast of Our Lady of Guadalupe celebrates the appearance of Our Blessed Mother to a poor indigenous Mexican farmer, Juan Diego, on December 9, 1531. Juan, a recent convert, was on his way to attend Mass at a small mission church outside Mexico City when the Virgin revealed herself to him in the guise and traditional dress of a native woman. This apparition suggests that Mary has claimed the poor and the oppressed as her own, extending to them her guidance, blessing, and protection. The indigenous Mexican population responded to her intercession with great devotion and loyalty, which continues to this day.

The following prayer might help you and your family celebrate the feast and grow in an awareness and appreciation of the traditions and beliefs of the people with whom we share this part of our world.

O loving Father, you have created all people
    in your image and likeness.
Sometimes, however, we forget
    the common bonds of humanity that we share.
Again and again in our history,
    we have taken advantage of our brothers and sisters.
Because of our differences,
    because of that which is unfamiliar to us,
    we have assumed a superiority,
    an arrogance that does not reflect your kingdom.
Our Blessed Mother,
    revealing herself as Our Lady of Guadalupe,
    challenges us to respect and value
    the traditions and way of life
    of the people who are native to this land.
Though we may be of a different culture
    and speak a different language,
    our shared humanity marks us all as your people.
We pray for your blessing on all of us.
Grant that we might be tolerant
    as we seek to grow in understanding of one another.
Bless this meal that we share,
    making it a sign of your kingdom among us.
R. Amen.

8. Solemnity of the Birth of Our Lord (Christmas, December 25)

There is no other day in the Christian calendar that evokes more memories and expectations than Christmas. Though Easter is the defining Christian celebration, the core of our belief and the center of our dogma, Christmas seems to capture our imagination and hold our spirits in thrall as no other holiday or season can.

Christmas speaks to us of innocence, of hope, of togetherness. Maybe it has something to do with the image of the infant, lying in the manger. The beginning of life always holds a certain feeling of expectation and joy. Or perhaps it is because Christmas is a feast in which both believer and nonbeliever alike can find some common ground, something to celebrate together, if only the so-called "spirit of the season."

As you gather your family, your friends, those you love, around the Christmas table, pause for just a moment and lead them in prayer.

O God of our beginnings,
We discover,
   in the birth of your Son,
   in his coming as one of us,
   a promise of hope and deliverance.
Somehow we can sense that this is important.
We may not always believe.
We may at times approach life
   with a certain casualness.
We may not even always understand
   why we do what we do,
   choose what we choose,
   or act the way we act.

But somehow, in the birth of your Son,
    we are reassured.
Our hope is reborn,
    and the promise of something better for all,
    peace for humankind,
    seems possible again.
Bless us as we gather around this table,
    with our individual hopes and dreams,
    surrounded by family and friends,
    nourished by the bounty of your hands.
 Form us into your people once again,
     and grant to each of us
    the promise we find in the Christ Child.
R. Amen.

9. Feast of the Holy Family
(Sunday in the Octave of Christmas)

When the Octave of Christmas falls on a Sunday, this feast is celebrated on December 30.

However it is you define your family unit, today is a day for celebration. It is a wonderful opportunity to take stock, to count your blessings, and simply to look around the table and remind yourself of the gift of family.

O holy God,
Your Spirit first went forth
    at the beginning of time,
    creating life out of chaos,
    light out of darkness,
    and humankind from the dust of the earth.

When the proper time had arrived,
    you sent your Son into our world.
You blessed him with a mother and a father,
    aunts and uncles,
    cousins and friends.
Together, they formed a family.
Many times, Jesus gathered with his family,
    the people he loved.
Bless us as we do the same.
Pour out your abundant grace upon us,
    fill us with hope,
    bind us together,
    and keep us strong in love.
Bless the food that we share.
Let it be for us a pledge of your love
    and a promise of your salvation.
R. Amen.

10. New Year's Eve and New Year's Day

In the blink of an eye, we move from the end of one experience to the beginning of another. The old year ends, and a moment later, the new year begins: if only everything in life could be so efficient!

New Year's Eve provides us with an opportunity to reflect, to take a quick self-inventory of the year soon to be completed, and to make a resolution for the year soon to begin—all before the clock strikes midnight!

New Year's Day brings with it the feeling that all things are possible. A whole year lies ahead of us, vast and open, like uncharted waters. We believe that the year to come will be better than the one just past. We emphasize brightness and hope-filled expectation. We tend not to see the potential for the occasional passing storm.

The New Year's holiday is also a time for football, so recall the tactics that you used at Thanksgiving to gather the family together. You are going to need all the skill that you can muster to bring them together again today.

For New Year's Eve

O timeless, eternal God,
You are the Alpha and the Omega,
    the beginning and the end.
In you, all times and seasons find their meaning.
We are at one of the crossroads of life:
    the last night,
    the end of a year,
    the fulfillment of a unit of time
    by which we try to keep everything in order
    and everything in its place.
We thank you for the days of grace we have known,
    many times taken for granted,
    but sincerely appreciated,
    when awareness of our dependence on you
    comes clearly into focus yet again.
Bless your people this sacred night.
Bless the food that we share
    and the company we keep.
Guide our thoughts,
    resolutions,
    and memories.
Help us to pray in confidence and in peace.
We pray all this in the name of Jesus, our Lord.
R. Amen.

And for New Year's Day...

God of our resolutions,
You are the reason for our hope,
> the source of our inspiration.

As we begin this new year,
> we gather around this table.
> We ask for your blessing
> not only on the food that we share
> but also on the plans we make,
> the choices that are ahead of us,
> the decisions that are a necessary part of life.

Guide us in this new year.
Send us a generous portion of your Spirit,
> that we might walk in your way,
> be confident in your truth,
> and live in your life.

Form us, your people, into your kingdom.
Make us a sign of your love,
> a witness of your forgiveness,
> a people committed to the gospel.

We pray in expectant hope.

R. Amen.

11. A Meal Prayer for All Occasions

As promised, a generic blessing has been provided. This is the "no frills" prayer, like shopping in that section of the supermarket where you can't find a brand name, no matter what. You begin to wonder if it really is possible that something can taste good or be of high quality if it isn't in fancy packaging. Well, the only answer is to try it and find out. Perhaps the generic brand is what you needed from the beginning.

O loving God,
Revealed to us as Father, Son, and Spirit,
We gather together to share the food before us.
This food,
 given to us as gift from your loving hands,
 feeds and nourishes our bodies,
 and refreshes our spirit.
We realize that we have been truly blessed.
We remember those who go without,
 those who struggle daily to make ends meet,
 but who somehow come up a little short,
 regardless of their best efforts.
As you bless us, Lord,
 may we never take your gifts for granted.
May we respect and honor those who are stewards of your bounty:
 the farmer,
 the supplier,
 the worker,
 who, in a symphony of cooperation,
 make this meal possible.
We pray, in the name of Jesus, our Lord.
R. Amen.

SECTION THIRTEEN

Glossary of Key Terms

A

absolution In the sacrament of penance, absolution is the form (words) prayed by an authorized priest for the forgiveness of sin. The actual words of absolution are "God, the Father of mercies, through the death and resurrection of His Son, has reconciled the world to himself and sent the Holy Spirit among us for the forgiveness of sin. Through the ministry of the Church, may God give you pardon and peace, and I absolve you from your sins in the name of the Father, and of the Son, and of the Holy Spirit."

actual grace A help of God that enlightens the mind and strengthens the will to do good and avoid evil. Grace is always understood as a free, unearned gift from God.

Advent A liturgical season and a time of waiting and expectation, approximately four weeks in length, in preparation for the feast of Christmas. In the Latin Church (commonly known as the Roman Catholic Tradition), the season of Advent begins on the Sunday closest to the feast of the apostle Andrew (November 30) and is considered the beginning of the liturgical year.

Alphonsus Liguori, Saint (1696–1789) Founder of the Congregation of the Most Holy Redeemer, a congregation of priests and brothers whose mission is to preach the gospel, especially to the poor and to the most abandoned. Members of the congregation are commonly identified as Redemptorists. Saint Alphonsus was a prolific writer known for his works on *The Practice of the Love of Jesus Christ, The Glories of Mary, Visits to the Blessed Sacrament and to the Blessed Mother*, and other works too numerous to mention.

Arianism A heresy, usually classified as a Trinitarian heresy, which taught that the Son of God, the person of Jesus, was not truly divine but rather created. Another way of proposing the heresy would be to suggest that Jesus was temporal and not eternal, he had a moment in time when he came into being, which is a false assertion. The heresy is named after Arius, a priest of Alexandria, who was the main proponent of this false and misleading teaching.

asceticism   Christians under the action of the Spirit have adopted means of self-discipline in order to have greater union with God. True ascesis brings a growth in contemplation and love of God that fosters personal maturity and social responsibility. Asceticism can be exercised internally as discipline applied to the mind, heart, and will, or externally through fasting, bodily mortification and austerity. Newer forms of asceticism include confrontation of addictions to alcohol, drugs, food, tobacco, television, work, and whatever else holds the heart captive.

attrition   Sorrow for sins because they are hateful in themselves or because the person is shamed or fears God's punishment is sometimes referred to as imperfect contrition or attrition. Imperfect contrition is sufficient for the reception of sacramental reconciliation.

B

baptism   The first of the seven sacraments, baptism is considered the gate to the sacraments and is necessary for salvation, in fact or at least in intention. It is the way by which men and women are reborn as the children of God and welcomed into the Church.

The sacrament is conferred by immersion or the pouring of water on the person to be baptized and the required words (form) is: "I baptize you in the name of the Father, and of the Son, and of the Holy Spirit. Amen."

Bethlehem   Today, a suburb in the metropolitan city of Jerusalem, Bethlehem is home to the shrine that holds the cave where Jesus Christ was born. The shrine is located under the eastern end of the Church of the Nativity. The present basilica was built at the direction of the Emperor Constantine in the fourth century and restored by Justinian around 545.

C

crèche   From the Old French word meaning "manger," used specifically to designate the manger used by Jesus when he was born in Bethlehem. It is also used to designate any representation of the Nativity in which the principle characters of the event are portrayed. The essential representations would include Jesus, Mary, Joseph, the ox and the donkey, the shepherds with their sheep, and often an angel. On the feast of the Epiphany the three kings (Magi) and their camels might also be added to the scene.

Cristes maesse   Old English words *Cristes maesse* mean "Christ's mass." It refers to Christmas.

consubstantial   Defined by the Council of Nicea in 325 which taught that the three Persons of the Blessed Trinity (Father, Son, and Spirit) are distinct and separate but share one substance. Another way of defining it may be found in the simple formula, "three Persons, one God."

D

devotions   Any public or private prayer and/or worship that is not part of the Church's official public worship. Such devotions may include the Stations of the Cross, novenas, a visit to the Blessed Sacrament, and so on.

E

ejaculation   A brief prayer that can be said from memory. Examples are "My Lord and my God" and "Jesus, Son of the living God, have mercy on me, a sinner."

Emmanuel   Hebrew for "God-with-us," or "May God be with us." The name is given to Jesus in the Gospel of Matthew (1:23). The word may also be spelled "Immanuel."

Epiphany   From the Greek word, *epiphaneia*, which means "manifestation." The term refers primarily to the feast of the Epiphany on January 6 (or the Sunday closest to this date in some countries) and celebrates the manifestation of the Lord to all the world as represented by the Magi or the three kings (Mt 2:1–12).

examination of conscience   The act of reflecting on one's moral state and its conformance to the will of God; a preliminary to confession.

G

Gabriel   Archangel whose name means "man of God." The archangel Gabriel was sent by God to the town of Nazareth to announce the conception of Jesus to the Blessed Virgin.

***Gaudete* Sunday**   The Third Sunday of Advent, *Gaudete*, is a Latin word meaning "rejoice." A rose-colored candle is lit in the Advent wreath and rose-colored vestments are worn for the liturgical celebration. The "coming of the Lord" draws closer.

Gethsemane   From either the Hebrew or the Aramaic word meaning "oil press." It was the place on the Mount of Olives that Jesus prayed after the Last Supper, the garden in which he was arrested by the temple guards.

Guadalupe, Our Lady of   On December 12, 1531, the Blessed Mother appeared at Tepeyac, Mexico, to Juan Diego, a native Indian of the place. She requested that a church be built on the spot and in 1555 a church was erected. By 1746, Our Lady of Guadalupe was the Patroness of Spain, and in 1910 she was declared the Patroness of Latin America. In 1946, she was declared Patroness of the Americas, and in 1988 Pope John Paul II directed that her feast day be celebrated in all dioceses in the United States.

guilt   A state or condition of mind and soul that follows upon a personal, free, deliberate transgression of God's law; awareness that one has done wrong give rise to what are often referred to as "guilt feelings," that is feelings of spiritual unrest or discomfort. Guilt feelings, in their turn, urge the sinful person to repent and to seek reconciliation, and thus once again to experience inner peace. In contrast to true guilt, which follows upon actual sin, false or neurotic guilt seems to arise from a general lack of self-worth or a scrupulous conviction that one is almost always in sin.

H

heaven   The dwelling place of God and the angels and the place of eternal happiness for all those who have been saved; it consists primarily in the face-to-face vision of God and the possession of eternal peace.

hell   The dwelling place of Satan (devil) and the evil spirits of all those who die deliberately alienated from God. The primary punishment is the pain of loss; the deprivation of the face-to-face vision of God and eternal happiness and peace. There is also the pain of sense caused by an outside agent, described as fire in the New Testament (Mt 25:41 and Mk 9:43). Hell is the dire destination for one who freely chooses his or her own will against the will of

I

Incarnation   The central mystery and dogma of Christianity, the doctrine that teaches that Jesus is both divine, the second Person of the Blessed Trinity, and human, born body and soul of the Blessed Mother. Jesus became incarnate in order to redeem humankind.

J

Joseph, Saint   The husband of Mary, the mother of Jesus. Only the Gospels of Matthew and Luke mention Joseph by name. Matthew's Gospel tells us that Joseph was a just man, one faithful to the traditions of the Old Testament and, by implication, a generous and holy protector of Jesus and Mary. The New Testament does not mention the death of Joseph and indications are that he died before Jesus began his public ministry.

L

Liturgy of the Hours   The official cycle of the daily prayer of the Church. At one time, it was commonly referred to as the Divine Office. The Liturgy of the Hours consists of Morning Prayer, Midday Prayer, Evening Prayer, and Night Prayer. This daily prayer of the Church consists of psalms, antiphons, hymns, selections from the Scriptures, and writing on the Christian life and of the saints.

M

Magnificat   Mary's canticle of prayer and thanksgiving found in the Luke 1:46–55. The traditional response of the Blessed Mother to the invitation of the Angel to become the mother of Jesus, "My soul magnifies the Lord." Some scholars cross-reference the *Magnificat* to Hannah's Canticle (1 Sam 2:1–10).

mortal sin   From the Latin word meaning "deadly," the term mortal sin is synonymous in Catholic teaching with "grave" or "serious." A mortal sin is a personal sin involving a fundamental choice against God in a serious way, a free and willing turning away from God's love and law in a grave matter. Traditional Catholic theology has emphasized three conditions for mortal sin: (1) that the matter be grave or

serious; (2) that there be sufficient reflection or advertence or awareness of the seriousness of the choice a person is making; (3) that there
be full consent of the will, that is that one freely chooses to do what
one knows to be seriously wrong even though one could stop from
doing it.

N

Nazareth   A town in northern Israel near Haifa, the site of the Annun-
ciation, the home of the Holy Family, and the place where Jesus was
rejected. An imposing modern basilica, the Church of the Annuncia-
tion, is built over the spot where the home of the Blessed Mother traditionally stood.

novena   A word signifying "nine" and referring to a public or private
devotion that extends for nine consecutive days or, in less common
usage, for nine consecutive weeks, with the devotion being held on a
particular day for those nine weeks. The Church approves of such devotional practices, provided that there is no superstition connected with
the number nine and that such externals are used as a help to prayer.

O

O Antiphon   A song, prayer, or psalm chanted in responsorial fashion.
The O Antiphons of Advent are proclaimed for seven days before the
vigil of Christmas. They have been popular since the seventh century,
achieving their highest popularity during the Middle Ages.

octave   In Latin, a word meaning "eight." Also the practice of celebrating a major feast on the feast day and on the seven days following. The
entire period is called the octave. The liturgical celebration of the octave might include the use of the *Gloria* at Mass and the *Te Deum* at the
Office of Readings.

P

penance   Prayers, alms, good works, acts of denial, service to one's neighbor, and so forth, that are performed in satisfaction for personal sins or the sins of others.

Precepts of the Church   Obligations imposed on Catholics by the law of the Church; traditionally six are listed: (1) to participate in Mass on Sundays and holy days of obligation; (2) to fast and abstain on days designated by the Church; (3) to confess one's sins once a year; (4) to receive holy Communion during the Easter season; (5) to contribute to the support of the Church; (6) to observe the laws of Church governing marriage.

R

reconciliation   The act of reestablishing a damaged or destroyed relationship between two parties. Reconciling humankind to God was the primary work of Jesus Christ and is an essential part of the Good News (2 Cor 4:17–19). According to Catholic teaching, reconciliation with God after one has gravely sinned against him and reconciliation with the Church that is wounded by sin are basic results of the sacrament of penance.

S

sanctifying grace   Created or sanctifying grace is a created sharing or participation in the life of God, given to human beings through the merits of Jesus Christ. Grace is always understood as a free, unearned gift from God.

Second Coming   The teaching of the Church that Christ will return at the end of time to complete the work of Redemption and permanently establish the kingdom of God.

T

Theotokos   In English, a word meaning "Godbearer," or "God's forthbringer," a title used by Saint Cyril, Archbishop of Alexandria, at the Council of Ephesus in 431. This Council confirmed that Jesus is one divine Person, not two as the Nestorians erroneously claimed, and that Mary therefore was the Mother of God, not just the mother of the human substance of Jesus.

V

venial sin   In contrast to mortal sin, a venial sin may be described as a less serious rejection of God's love, not a fundamental choice against God, not a complete turning away from God. It is a failure to love God and others as much as we should, a transient neglect of God and God's law.

Vespers   The traditional name for Evening Prayer. See Liturgy of the Hours.

Vulgate   The Latin version of the Bible translated by Saint Jerome from the Greek and the Hebrew in the fourth century. This version of the Bible is the one commonly used in the Catholic Church and was declared authentic by the Council of Trent in 1546.

W

Ways of the Spiritual Life   There are three stages of the spiritual journey of the Christian. Traditionally, the three phases were described as the purgative, the illuminative, and the unitive way. The purgative involved conversion from sin and disengagement from the senses or material things. The illuminative phase entailed a deepening of one's knowledge and love of God through contemplation. In the unitive phase, desire is overshadowed by the love of God and prayer consisting of loving attentiveness in which the person experiences an intense union with God.

These phases are not rigid, distinct, or successive and are governed by the uniqueness of the person and the ability to respond to God's grace. As persons mature in their spiritual journey they may be at different points in their prayer life and have distinctive needs. It is helpful for a spiritual director to be familiar with the process of prayer so that the directee might be properly companioned.

Sources

Scripture quotations in the Advent Vesper Service are taken from the *New Revised Standard Version Bible*, © 1993, Division of Christian Education of the National Council of Churches of Christ in the United States of America. Reprinted with permission. All rights reserved.

Scripture quotations in the Advent Reconciliation Service and other Scripture quotations are taken from the *Christian Community Bible*, Catholic Pastoral Edition, Claretian Publications and Liguori Publications, 1995.

Examination of Conscience used in the Advent Reconciliation Service is adapted from *Making a Better Confession: A Deeper Examination of Conscience* by Con O'Connell, O.F.M., Liguori Publications.

Advent Family Prayers are by Paul J. Coury, C.Ss.R., Liguori Publications.

Advent Vesper Service and the Advent Reconciliation Prayer Service are by Daniel Korn, C.Ss.R., Liguori Publications.

Advent Wreath Ceremony and the Christmas Tree Blessing are by Francine M. O'Connor, Liguori Publications, 1994.

Some of the traditional prayers and devotions are taken from *The Raccolata*, Benziger Brothers, 1944.

Some contemporary meditations for Advent and Christmas are taken from *Daybreaks* by Paul Coury, C.Ss.R., Liguori Publications, © 2000. Additional meditations for the Third week of Advent have been prepared especially for this handbook, also by Paul Coury, C.Ss.R.

Some additional contemporary meditations are taken from *Advent Daybreaks* by Elsie Hainz McGrath, Liguori Publications, 1998.

Symbols and traditions of Advent are taken from *These Forty Days: Understanding the Symbols and Practices of Lent* by Timothy McCanna, Liguori Publications, 1992.

Prayers for Holiday Meals are from *Bless us, O Lord: A Treasury of Prayers for Holiday Meals* by Thomas M. Santa, C.Ss.R., Liguori Publications, 1994.

Prayer of Opening to Healing and Transformation is taken from *Praying With a Passionate Heart* by Bridget Mary Meehan and Regina Madonna Oliver, Liguori Publications, 1999.

Traditional Examination of Conscience is taken from *The Mission Book of the Redemptorists*, compiled by V. Rev. F. Girardey, C.Ss.R., Herder Book Company, 1947.

Advent and Christmas Visit to the Blessed Sacrament are from *Visits to the Blessed Sacrament and the Blessed Virgin Mary* by Saint Alphonsus Liguori, Liguori Publications, 1994.

A Visit to the Crib of Our Lord Jesus Christ: A Christmas Novena, Jesus, Sweetest Child, and Meditations for Christmas and Advent are taken from *The Mysteries of the Faith—The Incarnation* by Saint Alphonsus Liguori, edited and revised by Thomas M. Santa, C.Ss.R., adapted from *The Ascetical Works*, volume IV, edited by Rev. Eugene Grimm, The Redemptorist Fathers, 1927.

Some definitions are from *The Essential Catholic Handbook*, Liguori Publications, A Redemptorist Pastoral Publication, 1997. Other definitions are from *The Essential Mary Handbook*, A Redemptorist Pastoral Publication, Liguori Publications, 1999.

Guided Imagery for the Stable of Bethlehem is adapted from *The Stable of Bethlehem, Twelve Meditations* by August Roesler, C.Ss.R., College Press, 1910.

Traditional Morning and Evening Prayer have been adapted from *Hamon's Meditations*, Volume 1, Advent to Septuagesima, Benziger Brothers, 1894.

Contemporary Morning and Evening Prayers are from *Catholic Prayers and Devotions*, Daniel Korn, C.Ss.R., A Redemptorist Pastoral Publication, Liguori Publications, 1998.

The material on the O Antiphons was adapted from *Celebrating Advent* by Anthony M. Buono, Liguori Publications, 1992.

Advent Wreath Family Prayer is taken from *Season of Wonder*, Liguori Publications, 1997.

A Child's Prayer Before the Christmas Crib is taken from *The ABC's of Christmas* by Francine M. O'Connor, Liguori Publications, 1994.

Light for All the World is taken from *The Blessed Beatitudes: Salt and Life* by Bernard Häring, C.Ss.R., Liguori Publications, 1999.

Prayer to Mary and Joseph and Mary's Firstborn are taken from *Mysteries of Mary: The Fullness of Discipleship* by Bernard Häring, C.Ss.R., Liguori Publications, 1999.

Prayer to the Infant Jesus is taken from *The Model Redemptorist Brother* by Stanislaus Werguet, C.Ss.R., St. Louis: Redemptorist Fathers, 1932.

The Way of Bethlehem or the Stations of the Infant Jesus is taken from *Meditations on the Incarnation*, edited by Robert A. Coffin, C.Ss.R., New York: T. W. Strong, 1855.

Sources

Advent Essays: The Church Waits by Thomas M. Santa, C.Ss.R., are taken from the *Season of Wonder*, Liguori Publications, 1995.

Some material on the saints of the season are by Norman J. Muckerman, C.Ss.R., and are taken from *Season of Wonder*, Liguori Publications, 1995.

Advent Scripture Service is taken from *Manual of Community Prayers* for the Baltimore and Saint Louis Provinces, Esopus, New York: Mount Saint Alphonsus Seminary, 1971.

Prayers to Saint Basil and Saint Gregory, Saints Andrew, John of Damascus and Ambrose, and the Holy Innocents are adapted from *Byzantine Daily Worship*, Allendale, New Jersey: Alleluia Press, 1969.